They're Not Aloof...
Just Generation X

They're Not Aloof... Just Generation X

Unlock the Mysteries to Today's Human Capital Management

Michael R. Muetzel

Foreword by
Ken Blanchard

First Edition

Shreveport, Louisiana

Ther're Not Aloof... JustGeneration X
Unlock the Mysteries to
Today's Human Capital Management
by Michael R. Muetzel

Published by:
Steel Bay Publishing
6007 Financial Plaza
Suite 510
Shreveport, LA 71129

Requests to the Publisher for permission should be addressed to:
Permissions Department
Steel Bay Publishing
6007 Financial Plaza
Suite 510
Shreveport, LA, 71129

Copyright © 2003 by Michael Muetzel
First Edition
ISBN 0-9740700-2-5
Library of Congress Control Number: 2003092420

Cover Design and Book Design by Robert Howard
rhoward@bookgraphics.com
www.bookgraphics.com

For more information on the author, Michael Muetzel
www.mxmuetzel.com

Contents

Section 3 — It's about winning...

Foreword

I am pleased to take a few moments to encourage you to read this book. For the past twenty years, we've been talking about dealing with changes in people and management. It's pretty clear that all businesses in America today are operating in a state of change. It's also obvious that in order to survive, companies must change the way they operate.

Companies need to re-examine their structures and priorities, and focus on their people and customers as the direct paths to more efficient, successful organizations. These types of changes usually have a tendency to make all of us uncomfortable. As much as we might want to overanalyze corporations and concepts, the simple truth is, it still boils down to people. At the end of the day, you will win or lose with your people.

Mike's book provides a unique insight on the "people side" of the often-maligned Generation Xers. The facts are, these people are not better or worse, just a little different and often misunderstood by senior management. The first section of the book explains some of the interesting causes for these differences and the unique environment in which Gen-Xers grew up. It was a far different environment than we — the Boomers — experienced in our formative years.

But this book isn't just about Generation X. In the second section, Mike calls for today's managers to take an honest look at their own management styles. He asks us to take out our "management mirrors" to understand the background for our current management techniques as well as how we might be perceived by our Generation X people. These creative references on management styles will be a little different from what you have read in the past, but this author has always had a unique perspective.

The final section of the book provides specific programs designed to make your people more productive in an environment where they have active participation in the process. Mike calls it "Employee Equity," and you should read this section because it makes sense. Plus, he'll show you how to get this program started in your organization without spending a lot of money.

The book is written by a successful senior level manager, but more importantly, it's written with a keen understanding of what will make companies tick in the future. It's about maximizing the potential of your people. In truth, the book is about them, it's about you, and it's about winning. It's a strong combination that will make you think. Then, as always, it will be up to you to react.

God Bless!
Ken Blanchard
Best-selling co-author of
The One Minute Manager

About the Author

Michael Muetzel founded Mx Marketing, Management Solutions, in October of 2000, bringing a new sense of passion into corporate training. Mike is rapidly gaining a national reputation for the immediate positive results from his motivational workshops, keynotes and training programs. His unique style has become extremely popular for corporate and trade association conferences searching for new concepts in leadership.

Mike's management track record includes success stories in companies ranging from internationally recognized market leaders, (Executive Committee, Yamaha Motor Manufacturing Corporation), to small and medium-sized, privately held corporations. This variety of successful management experience has been an inherent advantage to his growing list of consulting clients.

Mike's areas of expertise in management solutions include changing corporate environments, management communication skills, and he is one of only a few published authors on Generation X Managers and Employees.

Mike received his undergraduate degree from Bowling Green State University in 1979, and his MBA from Kent State University in 1988.

Mike's community service includes teaching and facilitating classes at Christ Our Shepherd Lutheran Church, and working with the youth and high school lacrosse programs in Peachtree City, Georgia, as a popular coach, and sometimes not-so-popular referee.

www.mxmuetzel.com

Before we begin...

I recently heard nationally recognized author and speaker Doug Smart say new ideas usually receive their first negative response within three seconds. That being said, I encourage you to read quickly.

My second caveat is that if you are not willing to be a student of management techniques, then put the book back on the shelf or return it before you mark it. This management guide / handbook is not about academic definitions of Gen X employees, nor about defending their new set of values or beliefs. In this book there are no cute animals. No offense to cute animals, and I hope none taken. I hope it touches your heart, but it won't make you cry. The section dealing with definitions of management styles may even bring nervous laughter.

This book is about a conflict in ideology, about a cultural clash between management styles for employees and managers in a business environment changing in a way that was never forecast. When we were in graduate school, we were never taught how to handle these "new era" employees. I guess you can just add it to the list.

And if you think managing Gen X employees and managers is a tough assignment today, then I can tell you the next generation will take you over the edge and push your existing management styles to limits you never dreamed existed.

I find it really interesting that many companies, including many of my clients, spend more on website development than they spend on management development. Hundreds of man-hours are invested every year on the budget process, yet more time is actually spent on cutting training budgets than on developing them. Collectively, they spend millions on extensive surveys to understand the market, and comparatively nothing to understand their own employees. So, this book is for managers.

I have a qualifier; in this book I take the liberty of making some generalizations. Like you, I understand the dangers and bias of vast generalizations, but for the purposes of illustrating my points and trying to get past the layers of conditioning and into your heart and soul, I had to make a few. So please accept my sincere apologies now.

They say a picture is worth a thousand words, and people are more likely to relate to images than prose. The book is filled with metaphors and analogies about truth. Some are written a little tongue in cheek, and some a little more direct. Some you may see with your eyes, and some you will understand only if you open your heart. And some, many of you will miss altogether.

The book is written in three distinct sections. The first section deals exclusively with Generation X Managers and Generation X Employees. The second section deals with four uniquely defined management styles, as you have never seen them defined.

The third section deals with specific techniques and programs designed to make the Gen X Managers and Employees the MVPs in your organizations. I hesitate to call it the solutions section, but it will get you started in the right direction. It will give you a checklist for your existing management vehicles in relationships with Gen X Managers and Employees. It will also offer you programs you may want to implement in your own organizations.

The order of the sections is by design, with one exception. Chapter Five deals with the critical nature of the information in the balance of the book. I debated putting it at the beginning, or even at the end, because it is so important, but chose to close the first section on Gen Xers with these statistics.

Without robbing the thunder of the chapter, *the simple facts are that due to the arguably smaller population size of Generation X, and a return to smaller home based businesses, the corporate workforce may shrink dramatically in the next 10 to 15 years. Gen Xers will be in short supply, and Gen Xers may also be the managers in charge in these critical times. And this generation of managers will rotate jobs frequently. The anticipated shortage, when combined with the high cost of turnover will force managers to modify their standard management techniques.* If you are in senior management or plan to be in the next 15 years, being successful at managing Gen X Managers will be critical to your careers, and I will let it go at that.

The book is short by design, and I hope enjoyable reading. Although the role of manager has never been more challenging, nowhere does it say you have to "go it" alone. And although the book is written with a sense of humor, it is a serious effort at changing management understanding and behavior. So, smile at the words, but take the illustrations seriously. This process has worked for other senior managers, and I hope it will work for you.

The role of management is to direct the power, open the creativity and manage the truth. It's about them, it's about you, and it's about winning.

And finally, this book is filled with questions; I will challenge you to answer them as you read on, and please respond honestly. At the end of the day, only *you* are going to know the answers anyway.

And I repeat, this book is for managers.

Has it been three seconds yet?

Section 1

It's about them....

Chapter 1

Memory Lane

Notes From the Sidewalk

As many of you, even those that are Generation X themselves, are jumping on the proverbial "Bash the Gen X" bandwagon, let's take a little stroll down memory lane. Put on your walking shoes because I have a history lesson you will not find in any college bookstore or collegiate card catalog. Many of the Gen X employees you see in your management and employee teams today were raised by the early-to-mid-Baby Boomers. And that says a lot right there.

Can you remember the happy days of elementary school? When you were in, say, fifth grade, and just getting off the bus. How would you have felt if you had come home to a dark and empty house? Doors locked; nobody home. Talk about panic. Well, this generation was the first generation that was raised, by design, to come home from school to an empty house. *Difference Number One.*

Their days started to the ringing of their own personal alarm clocks. Many began their childhoods in pre-schools, day care facilities and two-year kindergartens before even thinking about elementary school.

They came from either single parent households or homes in which the father and mother both worked during the day. They were enrolled in after-school programs until reaching the age of 10 or 11, when they were encouraged to begin their independence.

As they grew through their adolescence, they continued to return home to an empty house or possibly a babysitter, prepared their own snacks and started on their homework or chores around the household. We expected them to be responsible and independent. Those in early-to-mid-teens may have had the responsibility of getting their siblings situated after school as well. And this was also the first generation exposed to the electronic babysitter, the VCR.

More often than not, the family schedules required an air-traffic control plan, and the concept of a family dinner was something that showed up every few weeks on *The Cosby Show*. On those rare occasions when the family did gather together, the conversation might have been about Uncle Jack or even Dad being laid off due to something called an LBO, and their favorite baseball hero going to another city due to something called free agency. Talk about loyalty. *Difference Number Two.*

Or even worse, the family was being transferred again or Dad was considering taking a new job in a new place far away from familiar friends and schools. If you and your family have ever lived through this traumatic experience through the eyes of a child, you know what I mean. I know because I lived it too.

Speaking of trauma, what if I told you that in this generation, 40% were raised in single parent households[1], and Gen Exers were four to five times more likely to have experienced divorce in their families than their Boomer predecessors.[2] This according to Geoffrey T. Holtz in his 1997 book, *Welcome to the Jungle, The Why Behind Generation X*. Talk about living through trauma. *Difference Number Three.*

Many of us have been through these awful periods up close and personal; we single-handedly kept the therapists in business. Now take those same feelings of anxiety and spread them across the entire culture or environment. That was the world of the Gen X children. Wow. Can you begin to understand their lack of trust in traditional institutions, or their desensitized skeptic attitude toward those institutions?

Let's move on, shall we? The radio played lyrics from songs like Chapin's: "When you coming home Dad, I don't know when, but we'll get together then..." The same guy that was President also appeared on black and white movies occasionally, at Notre Dame of all places. What is a Gipper anyway?

You and I watched and cheered as John Wayne ate apple pie and conquered the enemy in sensationalized war movies. The Gen Exers watched television shows like "M*A*S*H" represent war in a much different light and questioned a government that was seemingly insensitive to the brutalities of human conflicts.

The nightly news always had a new feature story about a television evangelist or politician playing by a new set of rules, both morally as well as legally. But it really did not seem to matter to anybody. Maybe they were not real people anyway or maybe new rules were becoming the new norm. *Difference Number Four.*

People seemed to like to bash the Japanese, en route to the BMW dealership. No-fault divorce was available at the K Mart right next to the M&M's, and no-fault insurance was on the shelf highlighted by the blue light special. Then Mr. Johnson's local hardware store on the corner was demolished to build something called a self-service gas station.

This station was torn down and replaced by a fancy drug store. I am not sure why because medical prescriptions were available at the drive-through window at the grocery store, or on the Internet. In the store windows, Christmas became "X-mas" and Christmas carols were sung between commercials on television by the Jackson 5.

The old way was being replaced by the new way. OK, so I may have gone too far, but you get the point. We raised them to be self-sufficient, we expected them to be independent, and we rewarded them with even more responsibilities. They grew up under an umbrella of traditional institutions, in a hailstorm of inconsistencies.

Now Compare

I will take these issues to heart and compare them to my youth and maybe to your childhood/adolescent experience. Rather than an alarm clock, mom was always there to get me up in the morning. She gently, and lovingly, shook me two or three times before I would eventually wake up. I would put on the clothes she had helped me pick out the night before. And I would go downstairs for a healthy breakfast she had worked hard to prepare.

She would make sure I made it out the door to get the bus or walk to school. And unlike the Gen Xer's experience, when I returned home in the afternoon she was there with cookies and milk. She asked me in person instead of on the telephone how my day went, and was there to nurture my tender little ego with a fresh Band-Aid. Need I continue?

I had but only four grandparents, rather than eight, and they lived in the same town, instead of the same country. We visited by cars, not airplanes. We celebrated Christmas in the same house in which I woke up in every morning with only two parents as opposed to two separate households with a single parent each.

We played flashlight tag until midnight outside and traveled by ourselves, without parents, on the streetcar to see the Penguins play hockey in downtown Pittsburgh. Now I live in Atlanta, and I would never put a 13-year-old on a bus into downtown Atlanta; that would be nuts. And a metal detector was something that goofy people used at the beach to find pennies in the sand, not a prerequisite for getting in the front door of my high school.

We had one or two televisions; both were color, but only 21 inches. Cable was new, but limited, and at least I was there for the early days of the male dominance over the remote. A computer was something that had its own room at Dad's office. The Beatles were singing, "Here comes the sun, little darlin ..." and authority figures, well, they *were* authority figures and were obeyed out of fear and respect. It was the culture of the day and it was tradition. It was what we were taught and what we knew to be true. You see, I am a Baby Boomer, and maybe you are too.

Now, can we agree that a high percentage of learned behavior and attitude patterns in adults are directly correlated to their formative years, whatever those are? So then congratulations, you just got your first victory in this book. You have known all along that this generation is different, and I truly hope that now you may begin to understand some of the reasons why. Have I illustrated my point in terms of the different cultures and experiences?

Chapter 2

Who are they anyway?

Perception

I am anxious to discuss the inherent issues of trust with traditional institutions, specifically corporate America and Generation X, but before I do I want to review the images and demographics of the Gen X Managers and Employees. Hang in there with me.

In case you were wondering, credit for the popular phrase "Gen X" is given to Canadian author Douglas Coupland in his book, *Generation X* [3], written in 1991. You may not have known that it is a fictional novel; isn't that interesting?

Some allege that the unique name came from a reference to an "X" category of people in Paul Fussel's book, *Class* [4], and some suggest it came from Billy Idol's British Punk group in the 1970s. It was further reinforced with the timely introduction of the *"Malcolm X"* movie, and the popularity of "X" merchandise.

It really does not matter; it is here to stay and all just adds to the mystique of "Gen X." Coupland's tongue-in-cheek novel describes the lifestyles of three wandering Gen Xers who abandon their careers and traditional values. They can be characterized as carefree, aimless and lazy. I wonder if Coupland had any idea of the magnitude of what he had started.

This is the first of many correlations between the word lazy and Generation X and clearly not the last. The author talks about their unique perception of values; one can certainly relate if one considers "Occupational Slumming" and a "McJob" values in the workplace. Suzy Freeman-Greene describes the metaphors as lower priorities on even the most trivial traditional material goals or corporate success stories and a desire for a simpler lifestyle. [5]

The adjectives often used to describe the card-carrying members of Generation X are not very complimentary, and I am sure you have heard them before, or quite possibly uttered some of the phrases listed below. Perhaps a young promising employee left your management team one day after you had invested in a training program. He probably left for 35 cents more an hour, after only six months of employment. I can assure you that the Boomers developed these phrases, as most Gen Xers never use the terms to describe themselves. Can you blame them?

Generation X
The Twenty-Something Generation
The Me Generation
The Lost Generation
The Generation Without a Conscience
The Thirteenth Generation

Yuppies With a Conscience, but Without Fat Paychecks
Baby Buster Generation
The Free Generation (G.Holz)

I did not dream up those descriptions. They come from the many authors and managers who have talked with disdain about Generation X. Although some of those listed can be described as funny in an ironic way, I can assure you many are not.

In a word, the "slackers" of Generation X have been described as lazy and aloof. Up until recently, almost all of the writings about Generation X have been negative. The tide began to change in the mid-1990s when, according to Gen Xer and author Merideth Bagby, "Writers started doing articles on how this was the most entrepreneurial generation ever."

Bagby explains: "We were left alone a lot. So we had to fend for ourselves. That's part of it, also we saw our parents get downsized out of jobs. We don't trust corporations to give us a pension or to be there for us."[6]

Reality

It would be easy to be drawn into a detailed debate about the specific definition of Generation X. And as I am speaking to a degree, in terms of a mentality as opposed to specific age group, I will not get caught up in that detail. I am asking you to work with me. Defining the smaller numbers of Gen Xers in the population bracket however, is and will be critically important.

Suffice it to say that we are talking about managers and employees ranging in age from their early 20s to their mid 30s, with a little flexibility on each side of the scale. I am assuming you have employees or managers in this category. The demographics are interesting.

Some of the details below are compared to the Baby Boomer Group. The generation following the Generation X is often referred to as Generation Y, or The Baby Boomlet Generation, or Little Boomers. Although according to author and expert William Strauss, they would prefer to be called the Millennials.

The specific years of birth for each category vary by author and resource. At this point, I would like to mention again that under some definitions the Gen X population pool is significantly smaller than that of either the Boomers or Millennials. Thus the nickname Baby Busters. But not all authors agree on the size of Gen X, due to the varying definitions of birth years.

The ratios of these population numbers will be significant at a later point in the book when we discuss the declining nature of the future pool available to become managers and employees.

Generation X General Statistics

Born: Early to mid 1960s through mid to late 1970s

Married: 55% with an additional
               7% living together [7]

Children: 65% of Gen X women have children [7]

Technology: They learn four to five new software titles
               each year [8]

Job Stability: Many change jobs every 18– 36 months [9]
Ethnicity: 32% are non-white (24% for Boomers) [10]

Childhood: 40% from divorced parent households [11]

Religion: 40% attend church twice a month
(Boomers 43%) [12]

25% have confidence in religion
(Boomers 22%) [12]

47% said church teachings were important for
personal decisions
(Boomers 41%) [12]

Were there any surprises in there for you? Probably not what you expected? Let's examine Generation X at a deeper level.

In the next chapter I am going to deal with a number of characteristics regarding Gen X Managers and Employees. The emphasis is going to be on developing an understanding of how their different frames of reference and backgrounds will probably force you to change ... Don't like being forced to change? Then how about "modify" or "adapt" your management style in order to be a successful senior level manager? No, I don't like that. Too soft. You are going to *have* to change to be successful.

As we continue, I am going to write about the unique characteristics of Gen X Managers. Many are generalizations and we have been through that. The potential solutions will be found in the final section of the book. So, as you read, please do not think I am letting you drift farther and farther out to sea. The advice and potential programs to help are on the way in the final section, and trust me: There is a method to my madness.

Chapter 3

Trust, are you kidding?

Many of the managers I have worked with over the years have used negative connotations regarding the Generation X. But at the end of the day, the primary issue is that Gen Xers are perceived to be aimless, without any loyalties to the company, the senior management group, or even their peers within the organization. *Why are they so different?* Have you ever had these feelings toward a Gen X Manager or Employee?

OK then; let's get at it from this angle. How would you define the term "loyal"? You have to answer; that's the rule. If it takes a while we will wait for you.

Loyal– Adjective, *Merriam-Webster Dictionary*

> **1** : unswerving in allegiance: as **a** : faithful in allegiance to one's lawful sovereign or   government **b** : faithful to a private person to whom fidelity is due **c** : faithful to a cause, ideal, custom, institution, or product
> **2** : showing *loyalty*

I realize I am beating a dead horse. Many of you have already realized the issues and know where I am going with this, but let's stay with it. Would you agree that any discussion of loyalty or faithfulness is predicated on a certain degree of trust? Yes or no? Well, then, let's define "trust".

Trust– Noun, *Merriam-Webster Dictionary*

> **1 a** : assured reliance on the character, ability, strength, or truth of someone or something **b** : one in which confidence is placed
> **2 a** : dependence on something future or contingent : *HOPE* **b** : reliance on future payment for property (as merchandise) delivered : *CREDIT*

Trust– Verb, *Merriam-Webster Dictionary*

> **1 a** : to place confidence : *DEPEND* <*trust* in God> <*trust* to luck> **b** : to be confident : *HOPE*
> **2** : to sell or deliver on credit

Here is the bottom line. *Generation X Managers and Employees just do not trust corporate America.* Imagine that! This is a significant different mindset from their predecessors and the Boomer Generation Managers to whom they report on a daily basis.

Trust in Corporate America

"What you grew up seeing, versus what they saw..."

And before you start responding, "but..but..." let me take it one step farther. If you applied the criteria from the definitions above to corporate America and the people running the state and local governments, what conclusions would you reach? *Maybe, just maybe, the Gen Xers are more intuitive than we thought.*

Let's begin with corporate America. Now pay attention closely: the critical difference is that you have seen the trustworthy, as well as the untrustworthy. Does that make sense? In the time period when you grew up, the corporation, or even substitute union, was a rock of trust. After all, IBM was "Big Blue" wasn't it? And GM, well GM and its affiliates put this nation to work, right?

We previously agreed that mental impressions are made during the formative years, didn't we? And would you agree the environments of the formative years were different for Gen Xers than they were for you and me? Maybe I am being too subjective for you; try this commentary written by Rebecca Ryan.

"Loyalty is dead. Corporations killed it. In the 1980s GM, IBM, AT&T, US West, and others cut 3.4 million jobs in the United States. Call it 'downsizing, right-sizing or re-engineering;' whatever you call it the massive layoffs of the 1980s and subsequent recession cut a deep gash in America's security blanket. The millions who lost their jobs weren't just 'unnecessary overhead;' they were Gen Xers parents."[13] Now let me ask you this. In the eyes of a child, who is right? The corporation claiming the parent was no longer needed anymore, or the heart of the child that still sees the parent as a trustworthy superhero?

This is not an editorial about the issues of downsizing. I am only pointing out that one of the many reasons Gen Xers do not trust corporate America lies in the legitimate frames of reference from their childhood. In many cases, the corporations were the bad guys in their eyes, not the good guys. If you do not accept this in its entirety, can you grant me half a point?

Combine the lack of trust in corporations with the fact that 40% grew up in divorced households. No wonder they do not trust the same things that we trusted.

Trust Goes Both Ways

I also want to note a paradox I have seen in dealing with Generation X Managers. Recently I was getting ready to do a workshop for a company in Florida. The location is not important; I only add it for credibility. It could have just as easily have been your office. How is that for personal?

In the process of interviewing the managers as part of my preparation and research, I asked a Gen X Manager how he felt about the issue of "trust" in the company. Now, to be fair, this company was in a state of transition and most of the responses to my questions were centered on uncertainties about mergers and acquisitions in the future. Does this sound familiar? His response was unique, and frankly, it blew me away.

When I expected him to talk about his issues of trust with the company, he turned the table on me. When I politely asked him to share with me a little bit about the issue of "trust", he responded as though he were relieved to hear the question. He quickly asked me if others I had interviewed had the same concerns about trust. But his response came from a much different perspective than I expected.

He suggested that his concerns regarding trust were about his intuition telling him that although he had performed well and been promoted, as documented in his recent performance appraisal, his manager did not trust him. He went on to state that – remember this is from his perspective – his boss was constantly checking on even the most trivial responsibilities. "He hovers over me like an angry deer fly, and he doesn't trust me to do anything."

All of us have felt this way toward our managers at one time or another. And although you and I may have been there before, it may be even more important for us to think about now. Would you consider this issue in the way you manage your Gen X Managers? Think about it; it is important because *from trust stems loyalty*.

More importantly, what if he left the company and we then interviewed his manager. I wonder what the manager's response would be about loyalty and Gen X Managers. Could this example be about one of your Gen X Managers? Want to bet that the senior manager in this story was a Boomer?

Now I am not suggesting that the inmates run the asylum. That is what managers do; they manage the business. However, in the past, managers built responsibilities from ground zero. By that I mean employees started with no real responsibilities and earned more responsibility through their actions. That was accepted; that was just the way it had always been done. Business managers were molded through a basic apprentice structure, given small bits of responsibility at a time. But Gen Xers are different animals, and I can assure you, we all live in a different jungle.

These new young managers have been managing responsibility since they were eight years old. They had more responsibility for their own safety, their own time, at age eight than you and I did when we were almost twice that age. Okay, it is a metaphor, but will you at least concede that they need to be managed in a slightly different way? If you do not concede this point, then your life in management is going to be a lot tougher in the years ahead. Call it *Difference Number Five.*

Trust in Government

I think I have introduced you to the issues and differences regarding corporate America. Now let's talk about government. I am not going to get on a soapbox about the improprieties of politicians. That is not the point of this book and frankly it would be too easy.

Suffice it to say, this generation witnessed events you and I would have never dreamed about, from the illegality of President Nixon's actions to the immorality of President Clinton's behavior. During the Gen Xers' formative years, how many nights a week do you think they saw the national news lead with negative stories about politicians or government policy?

They saw changes in the political images from the individuality of Ross Perot to the body-slam background of Jesse Ventura. I guess that says a lot about their perception of the establishment in government. And let the record show we are talking about Minnesota here, not California. No offense to Californians who gave us Jerry Brown dating Linda Ronstadt. Nobody here said it was a bad thing, just different.

And I mean no disrespect to any of these gentlemen. In fact, many sources agree that, in demonstrating their lack of trust in traditional government, almost half of the Gen X voters voted for Ventura. [14] Also interesting is that when interviewed, many younger voters claimed that had it not been for Ventura, they would have stayed home and not voted at all.

But let's get off of personalities – even though it is a monumental issue in regards to trust – and back to the facts. Maybe the next section will keep the analytical readers in the book. I do not want to discuss the merits of the intelligence levels of Generation X; that is too vast a generalization even for me. Let's suffice it to say, without taking into account SAT scores, this is a street-smart generation.

They grew up in an environment of instant information. Although it was really the next generation that had the Internet at its disposal, this generation had open investigative reporting on television and access to many types of information that we in the Boomer Generation just did not have. They have a tendency to think quickly and can juggle many tasks at one time.

Remember, every evening they watched television reporters ask pointed, opinionated questions to authority figures. The reporters were held in high esteem. It was the culture of the day. Now that Gen Xers are adults, it is only natural for them to emulate the behavior. In *their* formative years, it was accepted behavior to see national figures question governmental authority. How can we as managers expect to change the standards 10 years later?

Although Gen Xers are filled with a million uncertainties about the government, the most significant issue is the hot, sensitive topic of Social Security. For the past 30 years, every week on television, someone has been prophesying about the uncertainties of the Social Security.

On the subjective level, Gen Xers do not trust government in general, so many believe there will not be any benefits available to them when they reach retirement age.

You may want to call them aloof, but please do not make the mistake in thinking that they are not intelligent. The facts may bear this prophesy to fruition.

Can we all agree there are issues surrounding Social Security? Can we all agree it will continue to be a hot topic of debate for politicians for the next 30 years as well? Remember that the population of Generation X is smaller than the size of the Boomers, yet at one point will be carrying the majority of the financial burden in supporting the Social Security system in the future.

In an article by Carrie Lips (the Cato Institute), she discusses the fact that most of this generation "has largely written off Social Security—polls show that most Gen Xers expect the system to bankrupt before they see a dime in benefits. If politicians think it is difficult to reduce benefits, (or raise taxes) now, imagine the world in 2030 when 22% of the population will be over the age of 65. Without benefit cuts, FICA taxes in 2032 will have climbed to 18%."[15]

According to the students at the University of Colorado in 1996, Gen Xers, when asked about Social Security, responded, "They had a better chance of seeing a UFO than a Social Security check."[16] When I was in college, Social Security was in my Day Planner to think about around the year 2010.

Please, stay with me; I am not talking specifically about the Social Security system, but instead the government's credibility. For example, if your accountant suggested – no, let's say that he dictated – that you invest up to 18% of your income per year in a retirement program you perceived to be doomed for failure, what would your response be? Would you trust him (referring to your accountant)? And if you think this dilemma is limited to Gen X and you are currently in your early-40s, guess what? Can you say reform?

Let me repeat, this is not a doomsday essay but instead a description of the issues surrounding trust that influence the Gen X Manager or Employee. I have just scratched the surface by discussing political personalities and Social

Security. There are many other issues as well. From the Gen Xer's frame of reference, there are significant issues of trust for both of the granite traditional institutions we grew up with, business and government.

Bowden Story

Let me close this section with one last metaphor. I recently saw a television interview with the legendary football coach Bobby Bowden. Coach Bowden has had a tremendous career, and when he chooses to retire, he could well finish with more victories than any other coach in the history of college football. And I apologize up front to him and to you for paraphrasing as best as my memory will allow.

When asked to describe the major differences between the young college players of 20 years ago and the players he is recruiting today, he responded that 20 years ago, when they were told to run through the wall, they simply ran through the wall. For the athletes of today, usually bigger, faster and stronger than those in the past, when asked to run through the wall, they want to know why. Do you see the difference? After he successfully explains why it is important for them to run through the wall, they simply run through the wall.

The concept of blind trust in corporate America or even our government is gone forever. Please do not interpret the lack of trust as insubordination; it just is not true. So deal with it. Deal with it in the way you manage the Gen X Manager or Employee, or be left behind. I suggest you deal with it, and in the final section of the book, we will help with some suggestions. You OK with that?

Chapter 4

More issues and surprises...

In her article, "Why can't Boomers and Gen X, Just Get Along", respected author Joanna L. Krotz addresses the different sets of values, and quotes Jay Conger from the London Business School: "What we are seeing in Generation Xers is a different set of attitudes about the workplace. In a nutshell, they distrust hierarchy. They prefer a more informal arrangement. They prefer to judge on merit rather than on status. They are far less loyal to their companies. They are the first generation in America to be raised on a heavy diet of workplace participation and teamwork. They know computers inside and out. They like money, but they also want balance in their lives."[17]

Other Characteristics of Gen X Managers and Employees

Independent

It never ceases to amaze me that we as a society seem to put the Horatio Alger candidates on a 50-foot high pedestal – just as long as they do not work in our management group or in our employee pool. Why is it that, when we interview candidates for an important position, we search longingly for unique characteristics, like Christopher Columbus, telescope in hand, hanging over the edge of the ship looking for a new world?

I had asked you earlier not to interpret a lack of trust as insubordination, and the same is true here as well. Remember as they grew up, asking a question about the truth in traditional institutions was considered the norm.

Hey, the fact of the matter is we, being the Boomers, raised them to be independent thinkers. Guess what? We did a good job. Now many of you want to change the course of the ship in midstream. This tanker-ship is not going to turn around.

Is it a challenge? Of course it is a challenge. Maximizing the potential from a team of Gen X Managers will stretch every fiber in your management being. Are you capable of acting as a peer advisor or coach instead of as a dictator?

I have to tell you that grad school for me was more than 15 years ago; possibly longer for most of you because I went when I was 30. Why so late? My superiors thought it would be the taming of the shrew. No offense to Kent State University, but I do not remember being taught about change in the business environment. This was possibly because nobody anticipated such a radical change in the characteristics of the next group of employees after the Boomers.

The days of taking a round peg and forcing it to conform to a square employee manual or culture are gone. I am OK with that and you should be as well. Remember, it is just independence.

Let me give you some examples. You may find yourself in an interview with a Gen X potential middle manager, and halfway through the interview, you feel as though you are the one being interviewed and wish you had spent a little more time in preparation. This generation asks a lot of questions. And occasionally they ask very pointed questions. Remember Bowden's comments.

"Bold and Brassy" are adjectives used to describe the verbal techniques of this new wave of employees. Remember they are often not concerned with office politics, or playing the game within the system. They are independent, and if that means going out and getting a new job every time they do not feel comfortable with you, well then, so be it, from their perspective. It is not an ego thing, just simply a realization of their independence and individuality. Do not be surprised we raised them that way. Expect it, deal with it, and respond to it honestly. That may be a switch, eh?

These not-so-subtle indications of independence are not signs of disrespect for your business culture but rather as a reflection of the culture Gen Xers grew up in. Do you understand the difference? And concerning independence in the culture of the workplace, if you are not familiar with the term "telecommute" then now would be a good time to look it up.

Aside from the probability that change probably makes you uncomfortable, what is the big deal if the work is quality work? You cannot hide behind the veils of past business rules if they do not contribute to the bottom line. This generation was born with X-ray glasses that enable them to see through rules and existing policies that do not serve a purpose directly contributing to the bottom line.

I have spent a lot time trying to convince you of the merits of modifying your management style to deal with this high level of individualism. You may be thinking this: What about teamwork, or teambuilding concepts for Gen Xers and other team-oriented business buzz words that have become the vogue of the past 10 years.

Teams

The camp is almost equally divided on the prospects of the Gen Xers fitting into team management. On the negative side there is that all-powerful "individual spirit" thing going on, not to mention their perceived shortfall on the key element of trust necessary for teams to be really successful. On the positive side, this generation has been working and playing in teams since they were toddlers.

They were in play-school teams, and after-school teams; even their high school classes were often broken into teams. They did not hang out at home with Mom and Dad because we were not there. They spent their time talking on the telephone and hanging out with their friends, even back to elementary school.

I firmly believe that Gen Xers function extremely well in teams. But I must make a few disclaimers. The first is honesty and those X-ray glasses I talked about. Remember the trust issue in regard to corporate edicts and direct downward communication. The Gen Xer will interpret corporate edicts as the same old establishment.

If the Gen Xer is allowed to contribute toward the vision as well as the process, then the chances of being successful will increase dramatically. You may want to read that last sentence one more time. The needs of individualism, creativity and responsibility can be met within the framework of a team environment. This is if– and it is a big–"if"– the teams are managed appropriately.

The Gen Xer needs, listen to me; *the Gen Xer needs to have ownership in the process.* In my other writings, I describe this concept as *"Employee Equity."* I am not talking about a stock option plan, but ownership in the process. Do you understand? Project management, employee equity and creativity in the process are all essential elements in a successful team made up of Gen X Employees.

Secondly, if the team has honesty in mission and purpose, then I believe the Gen Xer will excel in this environment. Stop trying to guide this missile. It has its own sensors and they are extremely powerful. Remember, equity in the process is critical, and you will read it again. Maybe that is *Difference Number Six*.

Transient, Some Might Call it Flexible

This generation of workers can be very transient. And in this context the definition goes beyond the traditional meaning of moving from place to place. They may decide to pick up and move on a whim or at any moment. As a manger you may not be able to control that, so don't try to control it.

What you can control is how it changes the way you manage people. I am suggesting you look at the employee or manager as any other asset. In the scope of the word transient, Generation X Workers may feel the need to move around within the same organization purely as a need to change. If the employee is bright and dedicated, do not be intimidated by their need to move. In the future, this type of employee could possibly be used in a number of different departments within the same organization. Remember they are lightning-quick learners.

The mission of the company is not to keep people chained in one place. The mission is to satisfy customers and generate a return on investment that is higher than the interest in your child's savings account.

This is not the way corporations have operated in the past, and I understand that. But if the talent has talent, as well as a short attention span, then manage it. That is what you get paid to do. And I would submit to you that the concept is not as foreign as you initially thought. No pun intended as you continue to read below.

I worked for more than eight years in management for Yamaha Motor Corporation. It was very unsettling to me to have had five different managers in eight years. Some changes were due to what you and I might call normal situations, and some were due to the inherent Japanese business culture of the organization.

In Japanese companies it is entirely normal for senior management and their teams to rotate to different companies every three to five years or so, all under the mother ship. In other words, a manager may work at the plant in Atlanta, Georgia, manufacturing golf cars and ATVs for four years. Then the same manager may be relocated back to Japan, for three years, then off to a bicycle plant in France. Three countries, three different job descriptions, three radically different markets and three sets of worker bee employees in a 10-year span.

The Japanese corporate culture places the emphasis on the job description, and the position, rather than the individual. As a matter of fact, the mission of the corporation remains paramount, and the individuals are merely pieces in the puzzle. Based on my experience, it would be nearly impossible for an employee to stay in the same group and same location from year one, and work his or her way to the top of that same group 20 years later.

In America we would say that same executive just couldn't hold a job. I have oversimplified the process, but the point remains. It works for Yamaha, and it may work for you.

One final point: Most Gen Xers are more receptive to women in management. They grew up believing in equality in people, not necessarily equality in systems, and there is a difference. This concept applies to men as well as women Gen Xers. Their world was different from ours in that their mothers were often in the workplace everyday. And their college and graduate school classrooms often had more women than men. Yes, even in the School of Business.

So the moral to the story is do not be afraid to try new concepts in managing Gen X Employees but rather play to their strengths and characteristics. We know they are independent, we know they are multi-task oriented and we know they are transient. Use these characteristics to your advantage. These "new" ideas may not be as foreign as you think.

Quick Learners Self-Taught / Technically Proficient / Computer Literate

This is really a key point and one many managers seem to lose sight of when dealing with Gen Xers. Simply put, Gen Xers taught themselves how to learn because often there was no one around to teach them. Let me give you an example. When we were kids, our parents taught us the sounds that a cow makes, "moooo," or the sound that a cat makes, "meow."

Gen X kids learned the sounds that animals make by pulling a string on that funky round thing with the animals' pictures going around the circle. They learned math from a calculator and learned structural engineering from a video game.

At the same age you and I had simple blocks or were playing army in the backyard or dressing dolls in the bedroom. In today's environment, if you play army on the way to school, you and your parents get arrested. I could never figure out why playing army was such a great idea anyway, but I digress.

Have you ever gone to your kids for help with a new software program or help on the Internet? I will never forget five or six years ago my daughter Melissa (now age 21) building her own website. She designed and constructed her unique website on geocities using programming language, not pop up windows. The site had colors, music, animals dancing to the music and so on. It was awesome. When I asked where she'd learned to do the programming to design the site, she smiled and said, "Don't know Dad, just goofing around."

I also remember my boss when I was in my late 20s telling me managers did not need computers on our desks. After all, his boss probably never had one, and neither did he. Now I challenge you to find an office without one. Let's call it *Difference Number Seven.*

I do not think this characteristic of Gen Xers needs a lot of illustration. You get the point. But let me ask you, how does this characteristic of the new managers change the way you manage people?

Sound Bytes

In discussing how law firms motivate Gen X candidates, Linda Green Pierce states, "But it is more than peanut butter that motivates Generation X. It's a total mentality. Unlike Boomers who learned technology as it was invented, Xers grew up with computers. They process information differently. The spurts of immediate information provided by computers and television has created a generation accustomed to getting information and education quickly and in sound bytes. That short attention span, which may arguably limit focus, enhances the ability to do multiple tasks. A range of available information through the media and computers has enhanced this generation's ability to draw conclusions from readily available sources."[18]

Drinking Horse Metaphor

There is the old saying, "You can lead the horse to water, but you can't make him drink." *In this case you do not have to lead the employees to the water. Just explain why the water is important, and they will find it, drink it, figure out a way to make it easier so that you do not have to bend over to drink, and take care of the rest.*

After you explain to the employees why it is important, within a week it will probably be ordered over the Internet and delivered within 24 hours. And you won't have to move. *But, if you lead them by the hand too often, and too directly, rather than let them find their own way, they will simply find another farmer. And we will whine again about the instability of the Gen Xers.*

More Comfortable Dealing with Peers than Authority

I will address this issue in greater detail in the final section of the book, but some of you may not make it that far. In sales training we were taught customers were more likely to remember what *they* say versus what *you* say. Do you believe that? It is true for the Gen Xers as well. Only they are more likely to respond to peers than upper management. They were conditioned by past events not to trust upper management.

Mentoring programs and managing from a peer perspective are not as difficult as you may think, and I will get to that in the third section of the book. Without your reading the next section on management styles first, I do not think you will understand the barriers.

So far we have discussed a number of characteristics for Gen X Managers and Employees. I have supplied you with information from my research on Gen Xer's backgrounds, frames of reference, descriptions and statistics. However, I have saved my favorite characteristic as a surprise closing to this section. In some ways I feel as though I have been defending Generation X, and that was not my intent, which was only to open your hearts to a little understanding of this unique group.

Surprising Characteristics

One way to look at a group of people is to analyze perceptions and attitudes. Another perhaps more pragmatic way to look at a group of people is to monitor the checkbooks. And after all, this is America, and everything boils down to the almighty dollar. So let's look at it through the rose-colored lenses in your wallet.

The first example is only a small snapshot of the situation and is used for illustration only. But it will surprise you. In a 1996 study done at the University of Colorado, (Cayman Seacrest,) Gen Xers were surveyed in regard to charitable contributions.[19]

I was amazed to read that over half of those surveyed had recently participated in some type of volunteer activity. The overall population statistics were only in the mid-40% range. It gets better: more than 70% claimed to have actually donated to a charity, versus the national average of around 46%. Keep in mind this was a small regional study, and I do not want to defend the findings nor put a lot of significance in the specific percentages; it is the indicators that are interesting.

The national figures are not nearly as high but reflect the same trends. The traditional inference with Gen Xers is they are selfish, aloof and out for themselves only. The data does not support that statement in regard to charitable donations and volunteerism.

According to data compiled by the Independent Sector, one of the country's leading resources on charitable contributions, the giving trends for Gen Xers are statistically equivalent to those of the Boomers. In the survey for 2001, under the category of "All Households", those who contributed in the age bracket 30-39 contributed an average of 2.4% of the household income to charities and volunteered an average of 7.4 hours per month. For those surveyed in the age bracket 40-49, the figures were 2.5% and 7.4 hours per month. And in the age bracket 50-64, the figures were 2.8% of income and 6.1 hours per month.[20]

Do the results indicate that this "aloof" generation, this "aimless self-centered generation" actually has a heart or even passion? And, perhaps more importantly, puts its money where its mouth is? As a manager you cannot channel what does not exist, but the surveys reflect there is energy or passion there, and we need to find ways to tap into this resource to make our companies more effective.

Unfortunately, for most companies, (allow me this generalization), the charitable work consists of who will paint the big red thermometer in the front yard. And, we offer to make giving less time consuming and painful with automatic payroll deductions. How convenient is that? This process pacified the conscience of the Boomer"– present company included – but will not meet the needs of the Gen Xer.

Next time you work on a "Habitat for Humanity" project take notice of the percentage of Gen Xers on site. And learn from it. At the risk of losing a few jobs with my own teambuilding workshops, I might recommend an alternative.

Instead of a ropes course, send the management team to a Habitat for Humanity project, or paint a room at a local Day Care. Your employees probably have kids there anyway. Go clean up a playground or volunteer your group at a soup kitchen. All of these projects will mean more to the Gen Xers and play to their unique needs and characteristics.

Many companies have already implemented this technique. Not only does it result in good things for the community at large, but is a great teambuilding resource as well. And it meets the needs of the Gen Xers. These companies may be your competitors. How does that make you feel? Do you get it?

Do not be afraid to take it one step further: Why not make the charitable activities a part of *your* corporate culture? This will then allow you to showcase these activities during the interview process. I believe this will not only help your company retain Gen Xers, but will also help attract them to *your* company versus the competitors down the hallway. And what is the cost? The cost is minimal.

See? You are learning something. And most importantly, you can do some good, for your company as well as your community. And possibly we will find a soft spot in your heart as well. Keep reading.

Chapter 5

Why is it critical?

Slackers or Managers?

"They've been derided as slackers, disloyal and lazy, but guess what? Increasingly, management jobs are going to these folks—Gen Xers—born between 1965 and 1977. Why? Do the math. The oldest Gen Xers are now in their mid-30s, prime time for assuming a first management position, and the ever tightening labor market means that even more Xers likely will get this nod." So notes author Robert McGarvey.[21]

This is a critical section so please read carefully. Let me begin by talking to you about your budget. Do I have your attention? Do you still think I am a bleeding heart? We already understand that many Gen Xers will change jobs at the drop of a hat. Can we agree that the cost of this turnover is expensive?

Turnover Costs

Have you ever taken the time to quantify just how expensive hiring managers can be? Are you afraid to find out? There are numerous sites on the Internet that will do the calculation for you: Go find one. And many have cost calculators that will help you in your specific set of scenarios.(For example, http://www.advantagehiring.com)

There are many more costs to the process than you might initially think. Beyond salary, and basic advertising, there are issues with severance, opportunity time lost, interviewing time, travel expenses, testing expenses, more opportunity time, etc.

Then there is the almighty learning curve, which I will discuss in detail in the third section of the book. Frankly, a middle management position will conservatively run somewhere between $ 35,000 to $ 45,000, just in replacement costs and expenses. Have you taken a look recently at the car your executive recruiter is driving these days? Now compare it to your car.

As a manager, you must analyze the current situation and adjust accordingly, sooner rather than later. So, first point: Our next pool of managers has an inherent characteristic to change jobs, in some cases every two years or so. Second point: The cost of this turnover is enormous. The third point may blow you away.

We talked about the Boomers' population, 70 million or so. Can we agree that most of these people have jobs? Do not get caught up in the specifics or finite detail. Simply put, do we agree that many have jobs?

Then remember that the Gen X population is potentially 10% less[2][2] than Boomers, and some authors note up to 15% less. *Regardless of the differences, add to the equation that more people are starting "stay at home businesses," more people are working solo on the internet, more are working in smaller niche related service companies and a higher percentage may retire early. So, can we reasonably presume that there will be shortage of candidates to fill these larger corporate management positions in the future?*

Manager and Employee Market Shortfall

Rebecca Ryan gives a short list of bullet points to describe the future environment in regard to the pool of employees and managers available for us to use to build our organizations.[23]

• A small generation of kids has grown up to be a small generation of employees.

• By 2006 two workers will leave the workforce for every one entering.

• The 25-44-year-old age group will decline by 15% during the next 15 years.

• By 2008 there will be a shortage of 10 million workers across all employment categories.

• History teaches us that when the labor supply shrinks, wages increase.

Not all authors agree on the size. Please, do not get caught up in the specific details of the numbers. I am attempting to illustrate *potential trends* for the future, not defend or argue specific data or percentages.

Now do you understand why this issue of understanding Gen X Managers and Employees is so critical for all of us? Do you see the correlation between this issue and your success ratio as a manager? Bottom line: Now that you have begun to understand the situation, and the characteristics of the Gen X pool, modify your management style accordingly, and do it today.

You are going to have to go outside the normal boundaries. You are going to have to be creative in the hiring process. Gen Xers read and search online, not in the classified ads. And you are going to have to be creative in your approach to retain the good managers and employees you currently have. Don't worry, it can be done, and done without breaking the bank.

In the final section, I will give you specific tools that work in many corporate environments today. But it is only worthwhile for you to continue reading if you are willing to make a commitment to a new understanding of traditional management behavior patterns.

Gen Xers are different, not bad or evil, as some have supposed, just different. We raised them to be independent and they are. They grew up in a period of our history when corporations and government were not necessarily at their proverbial best. So they have a lack of trust. Does it make a little more sense to you now? Do you understand their perceptions?

So with that in mind, it is time for the second section. I am going to change gears and discuss management styles. I hope you learned from this section and continue. But I am going to warn you that in the next section I will alienate some of you, make some of you smile and scare the hell out of some of you as we look into the magical management mirror at ourselves. If you do not have the stomach for this type of personal analysis, then just go to the third section.

I hope we have increased your understanding of Generation X and why they have the characteristics that so many have written about in a negative fashion. Next we will talk about understanding the different styles of management, as you have never seen them defined before. These styles are based on the perceptions of middle managers and Gen Xers. After reading section two, think about the perceptions. Are they reality?

If I have your interest, then read on and remember this book is for managers.

Section 2

It's about you...

Chapter 6

Magical management mirrors

"Who are you? I really want to know"
Peter Townshend, The Who, 1978

P lease, take out your magical management mirror for a second. Some of you may need to stop and buy a mirror. It's OK; we will wait for you. Or maybe you are one of those managers who believes that time is wasted on self-analysis. In that case, humor me and go rent a mirror. Or just proceed to the final section because you probably would not understand the next six chapters anyway. Sad, but true.

Are You... Your Father?

Grandfather Story

The other day, I was thinking about my grandfather, my Dad's father. Let me tell you, my grandfather was a very successful businessman. He was the last surviving partner of his public accounting firm. Possibly surviving on his stubborn streak alone. He was a tough conservative "old-school" German accountant. He started as a child laborer and worked his way to the top, without so much as a high school education. But was revered and occasionally feared throughout the local accounting and municipal communities.

He was respectfully referred to as the *"Father of Municipal Accounting"* in the many local areas surrounding Pittsburgh. He worked until the end, with no real thoughts of retirement or traveling. With him the characteristics you saw were what you got, period.

He had but one unique quirk. Maybe you remember, back in those days almost all of the breakfast cereal boxes came with "mail in" offers on the back of the boxes. Each featured a new "gizmo," gimmick, or toy. And this thrifty old German was addicted.

I can remember the twinkle in his eye, and the excitement in his voice as he proudly displayed his newest gadget. Thank God he lived before the days of the cable home shopping channels, or we would have had "Pocket Fisherman" everywhere. It seemed so out of character for this conservative living legend.

Now my father is also extremely intelligent, well respected and a great businessman. I love my Dad, but he must have genetically inherited the same affliction. Is that possible? He is also a "Gizmo-King." Most of his gadgets were related to golf. They too, had a life span of about two weeks before they were discarded to the garage.

He even had personalized tee markers for his full-sized practice golf net, and a real bent grass putting green in his back yard. He bought the green as a kit for about $45.00. What a bargain it wasn't. Do you need to hear more?

He had all the new training clubs, all of the new technology, and fought his entire life to break into the 90s. The green is gone, the small bunker is now a sand box, and he does not play much golf these days. Now he is hooked on the guitar. I wonder where that golf net is today?

I can remember laughing at the two of them. It seemed as though they were the two most unlikely suckers for every new fad. If you knew them professionally, you too, would have never believed it.

So here I am today in my office, three steps away from my "AB-roller," my "AB-DOer I," my video tapes, and my fancy electronic belt that shocks my belly so I don't need to do stomach crunches. If the truth were known, I have never used the one-year-old belt (scary), please do not tell my wife, but I bought two of them. And my slightly rounded belly, well I can tell you that it is still round but it doesn't look too bad when I have a nice tan.

Now, here is the moral to the story. Unconsciously or subconsciously I have emulated my mentors. Again, I do not want to get into a debate on whether this behavior is learned, or inherent. I only know, although sometimes I am not always proud of it, it is there.

Do you ever catch yourself sounding like your parents? Or, do you ever catch yourself repeating phrases you learned from one of your previous managers? Is it scary?

As much as all of us like to think of ourselves as uniquely independent managers, it is just not true. We are all products of our frames of references or experiences. Consciously, subconsciously our minds have absorbed the data, and then out it comes, sometimes without even hitting the "copy" or "paste" keys.

Only today, the scenario is different. The Gen X Managers and Employees will not react in a traditional manner. Quite the opposite. I am not sure we can change the ingrained conditioning of our past experiences, but we can increase the awareness of the different dynamics in place in management today.

Conditional Management

After reading about the characteristics of Gen X employees, can we agree that *"Fear"* as a motivation technique will no longer be as effective as it was on the past generation? After all, what do the Gen Xers have to be afraid of? Losing their jobs? The facts clearly demonstrate that finding a new job, or losing a job, is not intimidating to members of Generation X. Some do not even respect having a job.

Fear as a motivation technique will only work once or twice on today's employee, at the most. In fact, it may not work at all on Gen X employees, so please choose your spots wisely.

If you do not perform...then...

If you find yourself saying this phrase, you may want to change. Or at the very least change it to a positive connotation. "If we can accomplish...then this will occur..." Or ask the employees to finish, "What do you think will happen if...?"

I really do not care where you got your MBA, what your heritage may be, how old you are, what size pants you wear, or if they come in male or female sizes. I only want to ask you if you consider yourself to be in management.

Maybe we all need to take a moment and think about the *five most positive* attributes of the managers we have reported to in the past. What would they be? Then *score yourself from strong to weak on each of those attributes.* Our past conditioning seems to be more negative in connotation. What can we do to better condition the positives?

I can already hear some of you objecting. But that is not true in cultures such as IBM, or other staunch conservative cultures.

"That does not apply to us." I have a news flash for you. *The characteristics of the Gen X Manager transcend the corporate culture lines, for any business.* Time will prove me to be correct and you can't beat time.

Who are you?

What I really want to know is, who are you? Management techniques and styles have been defined and analyzed by many authors far more intelligent than I am. My categorical definitions stem from a different angle, a more personal angle, and come from my experience as a gang member in the streets of middle management subordination.

Maybe I need to start with a credibility statement. Try this: I have held management positions in small companies, and I have also held senior management positions in multinational conglomerates. I have worked conducting training workshops in industries ranging from cookies to cosmetics. I have seen the corporate ladder up close and personal, both from the top as well as from the bottom. I have been on stage in front of hundreds, and literally in the gutter by myself. And in my work with management workshops and my consulting practice, I have seen four basic types of managers. How was that?

And because it is early in this book, let's take the magic management mirror away from your face and point it somewhere else for the moment. I may have a better chance of getting my point across if we make it a little less personal. It will make things easier for both of us. After all, I think we are both pretty sure this section is not about *you* anyway. We will make that *your* choice.

Chapter 7

The Old School Managers

Old School Managers

A h, the old school is very familiar indeed. The Old School Manager (remember this is a generalization) is well groomed, looks good and carries the image of success as naturally as the azaleas bloom in Augusta at The Masters. He is usually a male – I am not sexist just realistic remember this is a metaphor – and gives the impression of total control. He personifies granite leadership and has the ability to put fear in the hearts of his subordinates by walking into the room.

Let the record show, via the metaphor, women can also fit this profile. The Old Schooler's inherent charisma is always present in every moment but can often be just as negative as it is positive. He is extremely intelligent, confident, great with numbers; he never considered strong listening skills as a prerequisite for success.

Let me make another observation. Did you ever notice the Old School Manager always walks really fast? I am serious; they walk faster than those around them, forcing others to a near jog, just to keep up. I really do not know why.

The Old School Managers are often older than their Gen X employees, but in today's business community they can increasingly be found in mid-to-late-30-year-old bodies as well. A 35-year-old manager with a 60-year-old's management style can be a very scary concept indeed.

The Old School Manager is a strong judge of character and makes decisions quickly. Interestingly though, the Old School Manager occasionally enjoys or respects an upstart disagreeing with him, as long as the dissenter has logic and strong reasoning and a little passion behind his new ideas. He has been religiously trained in budgeting and forecasting, thrives on meetings with the bankers, sends his boxers to be pressed at the cleaners, loves acquisitions, and goes into daily battles with confidence, and for good reason. As well he should; he can always out-walk the enemy.

On the down side, this style of manager considers management development an art form taught solely by him and those of his kind. Almost all good ideas come from the top or, at the very least, for some reason become better ideas when approved from the top. He has a constant handle on the pulse of the organization – or believes that he does. This is accomplished by figuratively yet firmly placing both hands directly around the neck of the company executives and managers.

He would never admit it even to himself, but new wave management ideas, employee involvement or equity in the process are fine as long as they don't go too far. Workshops in human development are like playing customer golf in that it is fine to let them think they are winning while in his heart, the Old School Manager is confident he still holds the power.

Old Schoolers feel the same way about organizational development changes. If things in the business are progressing well, and we are making the numbers, well then, pacify the managers and employees by letting them play with minor changes in organizational culture. It is like letting the kids play in the kitchen as long as they do not get too close to the stove. This is because the stove is for grownups only.

Now on the other hand, if things are not going well and the projections are not being met, it is a different story altogether. For example, if the sales group balks at un-realistic changes in revenue projections, then immediately out comes the strong hand of militaristic leadership, and trust me, there is no rose in this glove.

The first move is predictable: They dramatically cut expenses, including all overheads, and in the style the "Old School" Managers who rode into the sunset taught them. They either wield the sword themselves or pass the responsibility to others and simply observe from atop the throne.

However, this manager has a unique kind of truth about him, albeit often misguided in my opinion, but a truth nonetheless. What you see is what you get. Wouldn't it be refreshing if we could say that about every manager?

At least they are consistent, and there are no questions regarding authority. Because of this inherent need for power and authority, the Old Schoolers usually would be graded a "D minus" for playing well with others, at least in the business environment. But they do have an inner truth regarding their own blinding confidence that is sincere.

Although Old Schoolers are not really open to change, a few new ideas will be recognized and implemented when the ideas clearly contribute toward the long-term growth of the organization. The Old Schooler has no patience for middle management politics but recognizes an entrepreneurial spirit in subordinates and middle management.

I agree with authors Goleman, Boyatzis, and McKee in *Primal Leadership, Realizing the Power of Emotional Intelligence*, when they recognize the value, in specific situations of what they describe as a "Commanding" style of leadership. I also agree with them as they recognize this potential value especially in crisis and in the short term.[24]

I would add that Gen X employees may see it through the short term, but I doubt it. They will move on to another job, as this style does not fulfill their needs as a career choice. And following the Gen X Employees departure, senior management will again moan about the lack of loyalty as a common trait of the Gen X Employee.

I have just one other observation of the Old School Management Style. They like to beat on the mentality of subordinates. Like many of you, I hated it. I used to think it was just the nature of their personality; they were just cold, mean people. But I was wrong; they are far too intelligent for that. It is a conscious management technique. If you watch closely you even see a satisfied twinkling in their eyes after chasing trembling subordinates out of their offices with nothing more than a well-practiced stare. And some of them are just plain mean, and I will concede that point.

But when this style is combined with intelligence and charisma, employees take some comfort in the solidarity of the vision and authority. Because the praise is so rarely given to subordinates, they seem to crave it even more. In many ways it makes them work harder, thus contributing to the improvement in their performance.

It is like a militaristic, commanding "Bear Bryant Syndrome". Employees/players want to hate them during practice but have an undying confidence and loyalty to them as they head into battle. What makes it work?

It is based on trust. Employees/players must have trust and traditionally have always had trust in leadership, usually without reservation. This causes me to wonder about the effectiveness of this style of management in the future. As I have discussed in detail, one of the characteristics of Gen X Employees and Managers is that they do not have the levels of blind trust that employees/players have had in past generations. In fact, they have just the opposite.

Remember the story about the interview with Bobby Bowden when he said the difference is that after he successfully explains why it is important for them to run through the wall, they then simply run through the wall.

Now substitute the Gen X or Generation Y employee for the college football players of today. The Old Schoolers in the past would have considered the questions as insubordination. Can the Old Schoolers, or more importantly, *will* the Old Schoolers take the time and patience to explain the corporate strategic direction? It will be interesting to see...

Golf Handicap, Old Schooler

On the golf course, the Old Schooler is most often a really good player and thrives on the competition, like the family dog begging for turkey scraps on Thanksgiving Day. Old Schoolers are usually single-digit handicappers, and they are usually two to four strokes better depending on the size of the wager.

The reasons are two-fold. First, their will to be successful is so strong they make themselves good players.

They would not risk the perceived embarrassment to others as well as to themselves of not playing well. And secondly, if they do not play well, they just do not play golf, and that keeps it simple.

Although I have tainted the description, do not sell this style of management short; it made American business what it is today. And I mean that in the best possible connotation. Traditionally, this autocratic and almost militaristic style, with a little charisma thrown in for window dressing, has been effective. The Gen Xer will have issues with this style, in expressing his or her creativity and lack of input. But, the Old Schoolers get things done, and in terms of leadership styles, it could be worse; see the next category.

Chapter 8

The Old School Wanna-Be Managers

Old School Wanna-Be Manager

I have so much disdain for this management style; I almost cannot take the time to describe it here. Perhaps disdain is too strong a term. I do in fact have a degree of empathy for what I see as their weaknesses, and on a personal level, outside of the office, many are really nice people. But in my mind truth and honesty in management are essential, and the Old School Wanna-Bes just want to place politics over people. They play cards with a hidden Joker up their sleeves. In my opinion, they are clearly the most dangerous, and yet unfortunately the most common.

Some managers either consciously or unconsciously try to emulate the Old School persona and practice this style of management. The major difference is they do so without the high level of intelligence, skill, charisma, or necessary intuition to do so. Frankly, they try to be something they are not, and they just can't pull it off.

We have all worked for, or worked with, those who fall into this category, and if you do not know whom I am talking about, then look in the mirror; it may be you. But in order to keep it safe, I will be less direct. Remember, we agreed this is not about you.

The original Old School Managers are partially responsible for this debacle, as they raised and were the primary influencing factor for this style of management. Some of these Wanna-Bes are the same guys who were stared and glared out of the Old Schooler's office. You can tell because their tails are usually tucked between their legs like a scolded three-week-old puppy.

Consequently, Old School Wanna-Bes make great floaters as they avoid making waves in terms of taking risks in an organization. So here is a good tip for you: If you are ever in an airplane crash over water, make sure you are next to an Old School Wanna-Be in the ocean. Locate them and then grab on, because they can float on top of the waves forever.

For some reason, Wanna-Bes often speak in clichés and never seem to walk as fast. I don't know why. In the areas of intelligence and charisma, they fall just a mere tablespoon or two short, and with that the entire recipe for long-term or even short-term success is gone. My next point is critical.

One does not have to be the most traditionally intelligent tool in the shed to be an effective manager. That may surprise you but it has been proven over and over again, especially at the middle management levels. It is true. Moreover, the recent powerful research on "Emotional Intelligence" is changing the way we traditionally define intelligence in management anyway. It is about time; where have they been? But I am getting ahead of myself.

Unlike their teachers and predecessors, they either do not have the confidence of inner truth or are lacking in true self-esteem to the point of being afraid to let others see their doubts. The difference is that the Old Schooler has rationalized to the point at which he has no doubts; the Old School Wanna-Be hides behind his fancy nameplate or title and sees his doubts as a weakness that must be hidden like the last egg on Easter morning. Doubts and uncertainties in managers are not always a sign of weakness, as long as there are truths, and ultimately the ability to make decisions.

In his book, *The Five Dysfunctions of a Team*,[25] Patrick Lencioni refers to the "artificial harmony" in management teams driven by a fear of conflict. He describes a management culture that includes a fear of conflict due to a lack of confidence in honest disagreements. The same principle can be applied here in regard to the lack of truth in management, and honest worthwhile disagreements. It is just one more example of how a lack of truth in management can act as a serious cancer to a company and spread negativity and uncertainty throughout an organization. Say good-bye to the Gen Xer.

However, the Wanna-Bes are not afraid of conflict. They react just the opposite; they build themselves up by winning conflicts, especially the minor conflicts. Each victory reinforces the power of their title and demonstrates to subordinates that they have power. It can be so stupid and so obvious; I wonder why more managers do not recognize it. In many of these cases, the power play overcomes truth as defined by the best alternative for the organization's long-term success. And this is where it gets interesting.

Although they relish the conflict with subordinates, they often roll over when challenged by senior management. When conflict is directed from above, the power of the title or position is minimized, and since the inner truth or self esteem has not been developed, the issue is closed.

It is an interesting paradox; "their way or the highway" works only with subordinates, and the artificial power and confidence disappears when challenged from above. Next thing you know, the manager who just beat up an assistant over office policy is on his back, struggling like a dying bug waving his little legs in the air – no offense to bugs, of course.

This creates two interesting scenarios. First, if the upper level of management also manages in the Old School Wanna-Be style, then the circle is self-perpetuating. Do you understand that? And although we cannot really control this ominous circle of failure, we can bid adios to the loyalty of the Gen X Managers and Employees below.

However, the more significant issue is in the perception of the manager from the subordinates. When subordinates see their tyrannical manager as a robotic "yes man" to upper management, and a "no-way man" to the subordinates, there is further erosion in their trust and confidence in the management system. They may never vocalize it, but it is gone. It is yet another illustration of why truth and communication are so critical to long-term success.

Under the scenario above, the trust and opportunity for truly open communication in all levels of the organization is gone. The individual agenda of the specific manager has destroyed any level of trust from subordinates.

The opportunity to get a great idea for improved service from an hourly employee is gone. The opportunity for the group to work as a cohesive team is gone. That great feeling of a unit working together is gone. And with it, the best opportunity for the long-term success of the company, especially when dealing with Gen X Employees, is gone as well.

This style of manager, the Old School Wanna-Be, is willing to change under these conditions:

a.) If his boss says it is OK to change, duh....

b.) If it is politically correct to do so. This style of manager likes to read about employee empowerment and taking risks, primarily because they see it as good fiction in their day-to-day business management styles. It may be something they would like to see happen as long as it was not threatening to the title on their business card, yet they will never take the initiative to make it happen for the same reasons.

The Old School Wanna-Be Managers live for office politics. They love to sit back and watch others try to change the system and fail. It reinforces their false confidence in the floating technique of corporate survival. They have a misguided mindset that they know how to play the game as well or better than most. Plus, it gives them an opportunity to deliver all of those clichés they have been practicing for years.

Golf Handicap, Old School Wanna-Be

In terms of the golf analogy, this style of manager is not a great golfer. More often than not they shoot in the low 100s or above. These are the types of golfers who misrepresent their handicaps... in the wrong direction. I ought to know; I always get them in blind draws in tournaments. Bottom line: They will never be a 16, regardless of what they claim. A Wanna-Be is more likely to be a 28 masquerading as an 18.

But they are first in line to buy new clubs, especially big drivers. Probably a connotation or metaphor there, but

I digress. And speaking of metaphors, the same can be said for their automobile collection. Remember, we agreed this was not about you.

They really do not like to practice, don't go to the driving range because the solitude kills them. There is nobody to gossip to and nobody to gossip about. They just do not feel comfortable. They just do not get it. In silence there is truth, and in solitude there is only you. What could better epitomize truth than that moment?

But they thrive on the Saturday morning politics and "good ol' boy" stories with their peers. I ask you, who is better suited to perpetuate the mediocrity of the Old School Wanna-Be Management style than a flock of these goose-necked middle management office politicians.

This "willow tree" style of management will not be effective with Gen X Employees, even in the short term. They are too intelligent to be swayed by false bravado and already perceive most companies to be selfish and untrustworthy, all premises that are reinforced with this style of management. Imagine that; Wanna-Be's, losing credibility with employees. Maybe if they walked just a little faster...

Chapter 9

The Analytical Managers

Analytical Managers

nalytical managers are somewhere out there, although many of us are not sure exactly where. And I am convinced that is by design. They may share the conviction of the Old School, without the immediate decisiveness or clear-cut vision. They are often extremely intelligent. Do not mistake them for being weak; they too can trim an organization in a heartbeat. They do have inner truth and often carry higher degrees of empathy for employees than either of the two styles described earlier. The problem is they are not sure how to communicate it, and this causes them to come off as aloof.

An Analytical Manager is like a hungry database. They are skilled in preparation and have a vast attention to detail. An Analytical Manager may take months to make a decision the Old School Manager would have made in a few moments, as a "no-brainer." For this reason alone, they can be great for balance and an asset to the organization. They want as much information as humanly possible before making a decision. They always exercise sound judgment and will never be second-guessed for over reacting.

In most companies, the most paper, (metaphor), can be found in accounting or engineering. And this is the stable where many Analytical Managers are born. In terms of age, they can range from middle to senior, due to the fact that it takes a lot of training and time to perfect the skills of over analysis. They enjoy meetings, promote managers who write reports with lots of graphs, those fancy covers and 10 more copies than they would ever need. The tree huggers ought to go after these guys, and we would all have more oxygen to breathe.

To their credit, they encourage the group to assist in many of the middle to lower level decisions. They seem to need systems and defined processes for the flow of information; it fits with the organizational functions of the way their brain works. For them, strategic planning is best when done via the Arthur Anderson Planning Manuals. Spontaneous ideas are most effective when analyzed by committees for a year or two.

They do not like conflict and will find ways to avoid confrontation, usually by delaying decisions for the inevitable. Patience is a holy commandment; so much so that it often permeates their negotiating style as well. They simply just wait you out, or continue to analyze to the point that you give in so that you can get to your own funeral on time.

They may often see their intellect as an advantage and run you in circles until you give up. They are not beyond mind games when it comes to negotiations, even within their own peer group. They do have inner truth; it is just hard to get at the truth and almost impossible to get at the inner truth with any degree of passion. That is not by design; it just comes from years in accounting or engineering. OK, so that one may get me in trouble and I take it back.

As for the early metaphor about walking speed, they are not sure how fast they walk because they are usually wrapped in thought or dialogue. But you can rest assured they had a detailed map before they ever laced up their Bostonian Wing Tips.

Personally, I have always had a hard time communicating with these types of managers. That is my issue not their issue. At least I can thank Dr. Marston for his assistance in getting farther along than I would have ever been without his insight. You have to communicate patiently, in an analytical manner, and let them digest the data. You cannot convince them with your wit and charm; they will make their own decisions in due time. That takes patience, and that is where I am weakest.

Golf Handicap, Analytical Manager

Back to the golf analogy: The Analytical Manager likes to tinker. They have that arm up, hand-rotation-thing going on, and exercise good course management. No surprise. They may be guilty of extremely slow play, but not because it is their fault, at least not in their own minds. They may look at the yardage for five minutes or so, analyze the wind, the slope and what they had for breakfast, all before choosing the incorrect club.

By the way, their breakfast was probably healthy. This is also the type of manager who rather than engage in an emotional argument with a golf course marshal, will bore him with logic until he goes away en route to a five-hour round of golf. And all of those negotiating skills we discussed will be clearly evident on the first tee.

They too can have problems with Gen Xers due to their need to analyze over time. The Gen X Employee was getting more data off the Internet by age 15 than most of us did our entire freshman year of college, or in my case both of my freshman years. In addition, the Gen X employee wants to know what is going on, and wants to know now.

Gen Xers grew up in front of the computer, not visiting the card catalog. Remember in college, all of those hours in the library? *Well this generation believes that a library is a museum for information. Re-read that last line, it says a lot.*

In the minds of the Gen X Employees this lack of immediate communication is perceived as a hidden agenda and reinforces his lack of trust. That may not be fair to the Analytical Manager, but is the way the Gen X mind works. The Analytical Manager may be honest in taking the necessary time and analyzing data before a critical decision. But regardless of the honesty, this perceived paralysis by analysis approach will alienate the Gen X Employee or Manager. Communication rather than silence will be the key.

Chapter 10

New Wave Managers

New Wave Managers

OK, I know you have been reading and wondering. When does he get to my style of management? Maybe those mirrors are not working as well as we had planned, but let's move forward. I am going to let you off the hook momentarily; get in the easy chair because this is probably where you *think* you want to be.

Remember, this New Wave style of management does not refer to a specific age grouping, but rather to a management mentality. Many in this category are in fact older Gen Xers. If not Gen Xers, then there are many of us who think we can relate to the Generation X Employee due to the enormous changes we have seen in our external environments over the past 10 ten years. Not to mention the influence of our kids.

I think one of the first real ounces of credibility to the New Wave style of management came with authors such as Tom Peters and Robert H. Waterman Jr.[26] And add Dr. Charles Garfield to the mix. The fact that they openly discussed employee empowerment in terms of a new wave of customer service was a real beginning for this philosophical style of management. The fact that our bosses at the time, the Old Schoolers, were buying their books and listening to the new message was even more significant.

I can remember when I was in my late 20s, before I was re-indoctrinated into Old School style again with an MBA at age 30, when I had the opportunity to be introduced to Tom Peters, by Ken Melrose of The Toro Company, following Peter's keynote. With sweaty, nervous palms and a weak voice, I met my hero. I felt like the child at the mall meeting Santa for the first time. I could not wait to tell him how much I appreciated his giving credibility to our cause, all the time feeling like I had front row seats for the pending cultural revolution in management styles. The words barely made it out of my mouth.

I was a dreamer about the New Wave style of management. Then, as if without conscious thought, I got lost, not unlike the movement, in the midst of economic and corporate success. Yes, there were victories, and victories are good. And yes, there were shifts in employee development philosophies during the past 15 years. But the movement was subtle, not at all a cultural revolution, but rather a moderate shift in corporate paradigms.

Please read this closely. In order for a major shift in accepted management styles, there first needs to be a dynamic outside catalyst. The simple facts are that we did not have such an outside catalyst in the business environment of the past 15 years. Changes in corporate culture do not happen for the sake of change, not in a vacuum.

Unfortunately, even with the serious economic issues of the early 2000s, we still may not have an outside catalyst that is so significant and so dynamic that management styles are forced to change the way we manage people. These economic issues will clearly change the way we manage the day-to-day business, but let's stay on the people as an asset.

It is tough to bring about significant, meaningful changes in management when the economy is going well. It is tough to be idealistic about change when you are driving a BMW or buying a house your parents could have never afforded. I think it was George Carlin who said, "We live in bigger houses, but have less…"

Many times, New Wave Managers are really torn between the Old School Management style of their predecessors and superiors, and the empathy they have for their employees. The true New Wave Manager does not want his or her managers, or even his employees, to feel the lack of connection with the organization that he or she felt at the same career stage. For example, who listens to a young sales rep or manager with mediocre numbers regardless of how good his idea may be?

When does a middle manager have the opportunity to tell senior management, "Look, this just isn't working for me, and here is why, and this is what my customers are telling me…" without the fear of being accused of not being a company player, or even worse, being forever labeled as a whiner. Old Schoolers have no patience for whiners; so employees and middle managers stay silent, which further removes their emotions (hearts) from their jobs. They simply compartmentalize their emotions, and go back to the "McJob."

To their credit, New Wave Managers want to be part of a winning team, "team" as defined by *everyone* involved, filling a role, working toward the same goal. Do you agree that in winning teams, everyone works toward a common goal? For the moment, instead of the word "goal" substitute the word "agenda." Now look at your management team again. Can you say that everyone has the same agenda? *Without a common "agenda" the team will never perform to maximum potential. Is it a team agenda?* Is this too deep for you?

In the next section we will introduce possible solutions for dealing with the characteristics of Gen X Managers and Employees. But remember, at the top of the list we can put lack of trust in corporations, and lack of trust in government, and a basic lack of trust in anything based in the existing establishment.

New Wave Managers believe in satisfying the employee's need for equity or the emotional connection with the organization. New Wave Managers believe in open communication and are more receptive to change than any of the categories I have previously described. By now you are thinking that the New Wave Manager is probably akin to Cinderella. But for many, unfortunately, it is well past midnight.

But there are danger signs for the New Wavers as well. First, they can appear to their subordinates to be two-faced. This is an almost impossible concept for New Wave Managers to grasp. I know it was for me. They want to be the champion of the common man, yet report to General Patton. They may never realize that they cannot serve both masters, and usually, Patton is going to win. I am pretty sure he is undefeated going into the playoffs.

It is a little complicated, and you may not get it on the first try. For example, New Wave Managers try to be "Captain Empathy" to their employees and their managers while attempting to perform in the established style acceptable to their superiors at the same time. Can you start to see the issues? Secondly, the successful Old

Schoolers raised the New Wavers in their formative middle management period to be like Old Schoolers themselves, and that is what is expected, and that is what is accepted.

Golf Handicap, New Wave Managers

In terms of golf, the New Wave Managers are all across the board and are tough to categorize. One thing is certain; they are always late to the first tee. They need to check one more email before leaving the house or office. And then their self-perceived empathy towards customers and employees forces them to return that last telephone call before getting out of the car. I should also point out that the New Wave Manager is the strongest candidate for a sky pager for the reasons detailed above.

The New Waver cannot be necessarily defined by handicap range but can be defined by inconsistency. Seeing a pattern here? This is the player who shoots a 47 or 49 on the front, and then turns around and delivers a 37 or 39 on the back. Occasionally, to further demonstrate the predictability in their lack of continuity, they will reverse this process, and play well on the front, then hit it OB two or three times on the back nine.

To be a good golfer requires concentration and emotional control. The fact that this New Wave Manager has concentration that fades in and out depending on the side they are playing is a direct metaphor for the signals they send to the employees every day at work.

So, do the New Wavers have inner truth? Yes, most of the time. Good intentions? Yes, most of the time. Consistency? Well, that is where the pristine fabric of their best intentions begins to tear apart. Let me take it one step farther in the next chapter.

Chapter 11

Danger signals for management styles

Danger! Danger!

L et me illustrate this point with an analogy. Remember the story about my grandfather? Have you ever caught yourself sounding like your parents? Most of us have at one time or another. Although disturbing to those of us with a free spirit background, I guess it is only natural. We are products of our environments. Again, I do not want to debate the merits of inherent versus learned behavior, but let's agree that a lot of our personality and behavior is learned through frames of reference from our past. Are you OK with that?

Then, would the same hold true for learned behavior from managers who had a great deal of influence on us as we were getting out of our corporate diapers? This is especially true if the manager was successful and we respected that manager. Whether consciously or subconsciously, we begin to emulate that behavior when we find ourselves in similar situations, especially under pressure.

When golfers are under stress, they have a tendency to fall back to old habits. Habits they tried to fix because they were not consistent enough to be successful in the first place. The same is true with New Wavers. Under periods of extreme stress, even New Wave Managers often resort to the style of management they experienced from their late 20s to mid-30s, autocratic. This is where the real danger lies because unlike the original Old Schooler who was at least predictable, the New Waver is now sending off dramatically new signals to all subordinates in different situations.

In my own corporate career, I was blessed with great teams to work with and success at almost every level. Like many of you, I considered myself the poster child for New Wave Management. I was idealistic, and I was going to change the system from the inside out.

In my formative years of early management, I worked under perhaps one of the most intelligent managers I have ever met. He was also an ex-IBM Old Schooler. As I progressed to a major corporate position of responsibility, I found myself swimming in an ocean of multi-task management. I managed less on my heart and my feelings, and more off of my MBA, reports, forecasts and budgets. After all, this was the way I was trained. And unfortunately for me, and unfortunately for my employees, I was very good at it.

Like most of you, I have had some really hurtful things said about me in my career. Based on what you have read so far, you can understand why. There was always a grandstand full of people waiting for the day I would fall on my sword, they'd dance on my corporate grave and take my place in the pro-am. That's all right; I am always up for a party.

But the haunting comment that hurt me the most was from a warehouse manager in Cleveland, Ohio, Mr. Brad Sabrese, who had known me since my early 20s. Brad was a great employee. After giving him a new direction, I openly asked for his opinion, and to his credit he was willing to share it with me. He told me I had gone from an "us" to a "them." *Unfortunately, nowhere in the definition of successful teams do they discuss "us" and "thems."*

My superiors were proud of my progression, rewarded me with a corporate membership at Firestone C.C. and a "VP" title, and my subordinates considered me a turncoat. And in this frozen moment of truth, I still believed I was a New Wave Manager, but in fact I was a closet Old Schooler, again. How about you? Hey Alice, are you brave enough to look directly into the looking glass?

Actually, the scenario has repeated itself in my career, and will do the same in your career, until you open your eyes to what is happening. It took me a long time. Now I have learned that powerful, effective management is not a destination or a goal, but a journey. It is about truth and many steps. Can you understand that?

Chapter 12

Now, turn the looking glass around...

"He who knows others is learned, he who knows himself is wise."

Lao Tse, 604 B.C.

Who Are You?

*T*ake out your mirror, and rather than looking at it with your eyes, look at it with your heart. Do you remember where your heart is? Have faith, your heart has always had better vision than your eyes, and you are just out of practice. After all, have you ever seen a human heart with contact lenses?

We all are a compilation of all of the various styles described in the past chapters, in varying degrees. Some of us are just more open to admit it more than others. And that is my point. As we get into vehicles for managing the

Gen X Manager or Employee in the next section, you will learn they will see *through your mirror* with Gen X filters on their glasses.

The management styles I have described, each has inherent weaknesses. But is it possible the revolution is on the horizon? The strong catalyst for the dynamic change I described earlier may be the next generation of employees and managers.

This is especially true and even more critical when combined with the dramatically declining pool available for management positions, the fact that they change jobs often, and the high cost to the company every time an employee leaves. The employees of the future have needs and characteristics we need to understand and integrate into our management styles. This will be critical in order for us to manage them. Does that make sense?

For those of you who understand the sales process, let me ask you a question. OK, it is another metaphor. If you were attempting to make a sale, a sale of historic proportion, a sale that would in fact guarantee the long-term viability of your company, which would you do:

> a.) Address the needs you assumed the customer wanted based on the same needs the old customers wanted ... And use the same old presentation?

> b.) Or would you investigate, identify and sell to the true needs this unique, specific customer wanted ... Be creative?

I saw the master sales trainer Bill Brooks speak, and he reminded us that people buy what they want, not necessarily what they need. That short quote has been echoing in my brain as I prepared for this book about Gen X Managers and Employees.

Why is this principle so basic to sales trainers and sales managers, yet so foreign to our management cultures in dealing with our employees and middle managers? Do you get it? The stakes are higher than they have ever been before. In the past, we all got away with making employees conform, but in the future with Gen X and Gen Y Employees, I am not so sure.

Can we agree that we all want our businesses to be successful? Can we agree that we cannot achieve success and grow our companies without a strong employee base? Who stands on the line and manufactures our products? Who touches our customers on an hourly basis? The answer is, the employees and our middle management. Do you want them to be effective and successful at their jobs?

Why not spend a little time learning about their needs and characteristics? Then integrate these unique concepts into a management action plan. It sounds like a no-brainer investment to me. But many of you will only read and never take action. I am sorry, but it is the truth.

What happens when our customer market changes? Then we need to identify the new needs of the market and adjust our marketing plans accordingly. I can promise you, the employee base is dramatically changing and successful managers will modify and adjust their management styles as well.

The competition for survival is paramount for American businesses today. Ask the retired executive who has seen his 401K flushed away. Ask the millions who sat at home and watched on television as the employees filed out of Enron, and WorldCom, with tears and confusion as they carried small cardboard boxes and walked to the employee parking lot for the very last time.

Why is it that our management egos prohibit us from thinking that tomorrow it could be us walking to the parking lot for the last time with a box of personal items?

I cannot convince you to change your behavior or style as a manager; only each of you has that kind of power. And for some of us, even with the best intentions, we will never change.

But the Gen X Managers and Employees will force successful management teams to address their needs. And in the future with the declining pool, they are all you will have to work with, and frankly, there will be significantly less of them. In order to have the best chance of being successful, we need an open mind and an open heart. You see, we must analyze our management styles and modify them where appropriate, to give our companies every advantage in the world in the quest of being successful.

It is feasible, and we can do it, if you are willing. Who would have thought a quote from 604 B.C. would never be more relevant than it is today, and still will be for the next 10 years, when we discuss the next generation of management techniques...

Section 3

It's about winning....

Chapter 13

You want to go for it?

They're not as aloof as you thought, just independent and a little different. It is not your mission to completely understand them; nor do you need to be anybody's new best friend. You don't need to learn a new handshake or start listening to rap music, nor do you need to buy a new set of freedom beads or wear your Oakleys on top of your head all day at work. But you *do* need to understand their characteristics in order to manage them effectively.

You understand there will be a dramatic shortfall in the pure numbers of employees available to be quality managers in the future, and you understand that Generation X Managers have a tendency to jump ship like the venture capitalists at a dot-com revival. You also understand the cost of turnover is expensive and unpredictable. And you want to succeed. So the question becomes, how do we add up these new variables into an equation that works on the bottom line?

Are you at least open to a few new thoughts about modifying your management style? Where were you in the magical mirror detailed in the last section? (I am just glad you read it; you did read it didn't you? Did you get it?)

I am going to make an assumption that you did, and I appreciate the small glimmer of light you have given me regarding your open attitude toward change, and I understand it is not easy for you. Remember, it is not a destination but a journey.

Buckle up. And let's go.

Chapter 14

Employee Equity

D o you remember the sales training example, "People are more likely to remember what they say, versus what you say?" Would you agree that owners have more at stake than anyone else in the organization? Would you agree that basically speaking, people have an inherent respect for their own property versus property that belongs to someone that they don't know? Would you rather own the plantation or just work in the fields?

If you answered in the affirmative to any of those questions, then think about transferring the metaphor to your own individual management style. For this generation, it is not so much about recognition as it is about participation/ownership/equity. I will trash employee of the month and employee of the year programs in a few moments, but for now, let's stay on participation.

When the sun came up on your management career today, it came up on the other side of the bed. The new angle is about employee involvement in the process of management. But first, you need to understand Employee Equity. This is not about stock options.

Employee Equity is the involvement in the development – did you hear it? – *development of the systems as well as the process*, rather than just the responsibility for the implementation. We are not making them the new bosses, just getting them involved in the process. *You are still the manager*.

Many managers today, including the New Wavers, are proud of how they allow their employees to decide how to implement company policy. In their own minds, they are simply leading the horse to drink. In today's world, managers need to go beyond that principal to one of getting everyone involved in development as well as in implementation. This is critical if you expect to keep the Gen Xer focused in your company.

I am hesitant to give you this real-life example, at the risk of embarrassing some of the key players. I am very cognizant of the feelings of some really good people so I will change the names to protect the innocent, but I can assure you it happened. And it will be represented here as a hypothetical example, embellished for effect, as you have come to expect from me.

Equity Example, Technician Story

Once upon a time, in a galaxy far, far away... It was well past 7 p.m., and I was sitting at my desk as usual, re-arranging piles of paper on the floor to make the surface of my desk appear to be clean before going home for the evening. Must be a hangover from the Old School influence and training. Lucky for me, I still had some floor space left. I was a senior manager.

Anyway, I received a telephone call from a friend, a key customer, also a senior-level executive. I guess they are all key customers, but you get my drift; this one was special. He was respected throughout the entire industry and an asset to our customer base.

This is one of those customers who was not only good business, but also good people as well. Do you have any of those? I never know what to expect when they call at 7 p.m. I thought it was a little strange for him to call that late in the evening, just to tell me what a great job we were doing in meeting his needs and exceeding his expectations. I should have been a fortuneteller.

The customer called to express a concern regarding a service call made by one of our national service team members to one of his many facilities. The customer – my friend – went on to say he was still getting the details together, but evidently there had been an alleged incident at one of his facilities regarding a public shouting match between one of his general managers and one of our national technical service representatives.

It was reported that the language in this particular dialogue was creative well beyond the normal parameters of the Queen's English. As you do in your company, we encouraged strong communication skills and creativity in our employees at every level, but I digress.

In this particular case, I knew the young technician personally. I liked and respected him to the point that in my own mind, I had targeted him for advancement in the organization. He was a Gen Xer with potential.

He was well mannered, professional in appearance, educated, computer literate, good with customers, and so on. I also had visited the facility in question and met the local customer General Manager in the story. The General Manager on site was, well to tell the truth, he was a jerk. You know the type: a Wanna-Be Manager, "Mr. T" jewelry starter kit, etc. But as you know, the customer is always right, and perspective is reality in the eyes of the customer, so I just listened to the accounts of the story from my respected friend.

We both agreed to do a little research and talk in the next day or so. I had a discussion with the tech rep's manager; he was alarmed I had received the call. He was a little territorial, but calm, to his credit. The story, or alleged incident, was true. Our employee had gone so far as to point out deficiencies in the heritage of the General Manager, as well as a little constructive criticism on the manager's ability to accomplish tasks in a reasonable time frame. We are always trying to help.

Seriously, we were clearly in the wrong. The National Service Manager pointed out that this type of scenario had occurred at least once in the past that he was aware of, and suggested that due to the repetition of the insubordination and the magnitude of the importance of this or any customer, firm action would be required.

He wanted to talk to the young tech representative, but it looked like termination was the appropriate response. I heard that little inner voice in my head saying something, but after all, it was ultimately the call of the manager. I did not want to micro-manage, but the little voice continued nonetheless.

I returned the telephone call to my friend and explained what I had learned so far. And expressed my personal apologies as well as those of our organization. He too had a stable full of managers and employees, and appreciated my time and concern. This type of behavior toward a customer was not acceptable, no excuses, end of dialogue.

Over the next day or two, the voice in my head became more than a voice and developed into a nagging headache. On one level, I was concerned about our customer service across the country. I also wondered about the validity of our scientific and quantitative customer satisfaction index. Even the strongest reports can muffle a single voice of frustration. But there was something else bothering me. I could not put my finger on the message of the voice. I felt so frustrated.

Then a day later the voice decided to actually share the message. I finally understood what the voice had been trying to say. I went back to the National Service Manager. He had talked to the tech rep, and although the young employee felt terrible, he clearly understood the magnitude of his actions; he was a bright guy. He also understood that he would have to bear responsibility for his actions.

The employee had not yet been terminated, and in fairness to the manager, he had not visited with the HR Department to get the 17-page form to fill out and distribute. He had not yet checked on the status of benefits, 401K, etc. He was busy managing the business. I understood; I think we all understand.

But back to my point. The National Service Manager seemed a little surprised as I returned to his office that day and sat down. He was even more surprised at my comments. I suggested that before we fire the tech rep, we take a look at firing ourselves first. At the very least we should have been "written up". After looking in the management mirror, I realized we too were guilty.

We had expected this young professional to know how to deal with an unhappy-to-the-point-of-being-arrogant customer. The tech reps were expected to carry an enormous load, advanced technical knowledge, GPS Systems in the vehicles, computerized invoicing and work orders, etc. They often worked outdoors in the brutal summer heat of Texas and Florida.

They faced customers' anxieties over factory mishaps, and premium pricing for quality goods. Nothing worse than getting abused for something that someone else was responsible for, and taking it like the company man you were raised to be. Ever been there? Me too. Did I mention the factory was air-conditioned? We can't have the throne uncomfortable, can we? That is why we need insulation. Do you get the metaphor?

Have you ever tried to find strong people skills in an engineering type of person? Well, it is a similar analogy. Why does God make us that way? In this case, factory-trained, translated into technically proficient. I'd like to think I would have handled the situation better, but then again, my training is people, not engines and electronics. Or maybe I am just wrong.

Most managers would have fired the tech rep and then written a memo about the importance of customer service and the value of customer relationships. We decided on a different solution: Employee Equity.

Now, this is not a hypothetical story about customer service. It is not about an empathetic management style. It is about communication and equity in process and solutions. With our technical reps, we had never taken the time to really address potential negative situations in the field. We knew they were strong in service, and we knew that people who are strong in technical proficiencies are sometimes weak in personal communication skills.

This may be one of those vast generalizations and biased to the point of being judgmental. But let that part go. The first reaction of management is usually to chastise the employee for something we would have considered common sense. It was a good time for one of those mirrors, eh?

We all have a tendency to put the blame on the employee. "That damn employee!" But in this example, management was equally at fault. How does your conscience allow you to evaluate the performance of an employee, even to chastise an employee, against a corporate barometer that in cases like this does not exist outside of your own mind?

If we as managers never provided the standards of what is acceptable versus non-acceptable, how can one say the young employee did not measure up? I have over-dramatized the point, and yes, the employee should have clearly known better, and did know better, but the point remains valid.

Solution

But it is the solution I am most proud of. We quickly called a meeting of all of the national technical service representatives. There was an expense bringing them all back to Atlanta at the drop of a hat, but bear with me. The expense was minimal in terms of dollars compared to the cost of losing a quality customer or even the cost of replacing a quality employee. Do you agree?

We brought the tech team into one room. We had the young rep explain the situation to all of his peers, the tech reps from around the country. It was clear by the empathy in their eyes he merely had done what they had all wanted to do at one time or another. But it was still wrong, and potentially expensive for the company.

The next four hours were spent with the tech teams broken into small groups, discussing a new Customer Relations Manual to communicate and set standards for their important group. The manual included this and other real-life experiences, and they, the teams, developed procedures for dealing with each example. They identified the issues, they identified the solutions and they developed the process. In short, *they – the tech team – owned the solutions. It was Employee Equity.*

One of my proudest moments - you know what I mean - one of those management moments nobody else knows about but you, occurred three months later. Like the phenomenal bunker shot on 18; it was the shot that makes you want to come back.

One day when walking through the training lab, I noticed a senior tech service representative talking to a new face I did not recognize. In the spirit, I went over and introduced myself to the new employee and with a sincere voice welcomed him to the organization. I asked what they were working on, not that I really wanted to know; it was just an excuse to avoid returning to my office and a new onslaught of emails and messages.

The senior tech representative responded that he was chosen to review the Customer Relations Manual with the new hire. Please note that it is critical that a peer do the review and not a manager. And by now you know why.

"I just told him that the manual is really important and will really help him in the field. I also told him we wrote it, and re-write it every year or so..." I am glad he smiled, because I felt a lump in my throat. I was so proud of them.

Now, if you think it is about me, you are wrong. If I had any brains, we would have addressed customer relations as part of the technical orientation process from day one. I would have recognized that these reps spent more "face" time with our valued customers than anyone from management. If I had any brains, I would have had a system developed by the internal experts in the field before my friend ever called that night at 7.

They call it Employee Equity. It was easy, once my ego was on the shelf. I was lucky to have a national manager who was also open to new ideas. The cost was minimal, especially compared to the alternatives. And no consultant in America could have done what that team did in that room in four hours. Yes, management typed it up nice and pretty, we had it spiral bound, and yes, we had all of the authors sign the last page before going to print. After all, they wrote it. After all, they owned it.

Were there other issues? Yes, there were other issues, but the impetus was not on management for being the ominous customer relations police; the tech team now had to answer to their peers. And in my wildest dreams, in my best blue tights and red cape, (I look good in capes) I could never reach that level of power. Employee Equity; do you get it? And more importantly, how can you use it? *How did you like that touch of having them sign the last page before going to print?*

Guess what? *There was no additional cost for the personal signature page, but the value of the manual increased significantly.* Do you agree?

Chapter 15

Vehicles, the elements to be successful

Promises

I promised you a checklist, and I promised you some examples of employee programs you could use as templates in your own organization. Instead of checklists, let's use the term "vehicles". And I will deliver, but I proceed with caution. Although it may be perceived as a potential negative, I am going to begin this chapter with a disclaimer.

The new Gen X Managers will see antique "old-style" employee programs to be archaic vehicles developed to serve the needs of a traditional management structure. I am referring to the same institutional structures they saw as "artificial", or self-serving, in their – the Gen Xer's – formative years. These are the same institutions that cost "heroes" their jobs and security in the late 1970s and 1980s.

Remember there are no rules, although you may think there are, or think there have to be, regarding the involvement of Gen Xers in the development of their own programs. As a matter of fact, I hope by now you see the advantages in such a philosophy, as well as the savings, in letting them have the "equity" in the process of program development.

And although your programs may need to be customized, I want to discuss some common, basic ingredients that the programs need to have in place before they can be successful. This is a subtle distinction; please consider the points carefully.

What's a vehicle?

Now that you are beginning to understand the characteristics of Gen X Managers and Employees, you need to understand the need for vehicles. I chose the term vehicle because of the inherent connotation of travel. In terms of management styles we are trying to go from one place to another place to accomplish a common good. Some use the term conduit, but a conduit remains externally stationary, only housing the moving vehicles. Too deep for you? It's OK.

We are talking about programs, or potential programs, that instill motivation and interest and, in this case, improve the rates of employee retention. Employee retention is a giant issue, and retention will become more critical in the years ahead for reasons we have already covered in detail.

Employee motivation requires communication, and communication requires a vehicle. You have to have a vehicle, or vehicles, in order to be successful motivating Gen X Managers. The vehicle is made up of systems and training. The vehicles can also be used as tools for problem solving as well, as discussed in Chapter 14. For the time being, let's concentrate on communication.

Many of you are going to have a problem initially with this concept because it cannot be quantified in the short term. In that aspect, it is very similar to management training. Old School Managers and Wanna-Bes will scoff at the concept until the retention issue, acting as that important outside catalyst for change, demands attention. However, due to the "pick up and leave" characteristics of Gen Xers, we will be able to measure the retention statistics sooner rather than later.

If I am losing you due to what you see as "Liberal Management 101", let me continue. Almost all corporations keep statistics on safety records, line pitch rates, QA inspection ratios, and yes, even employee retention statistics. I would be curious to know what the statistics are in your organization for retention of Gen Xers versus Boomers. I know you are going to argue that younger people are unstable, leave daily for a better nightlife, or due to a pending drug exam.

Get your head out of the sand and start to look at retention rates for Gen Xers as a unique category, if for no other reason than to prove me wrong. But I won't be wrong. And remember, as the workforce pool shrinks in size, wages and replacement costs will escalate. Can I convince you to consider change on the basis of cost effectiveness?

And if I cannot hook you with the philosophical angle, let's talk about productivity. Do you think satisfied employees are more productive? Is this a little too much "New Wave" for you? Don't take my word for it. There are now statistics and research that confirm this statement.

If you have not read any of the work by Daniel Goleman, Richard Boyatzis and Annie McKee, *Primal Leadership, Realizing the Power of Emotional Intelligence*, is a good place to start. *Primal Leadership* quotes a number of resources which studied the effect of employee attitude on productivity. As early as the first chapter, they quote from a report from Lyle Spencer, published more than 10 years ago.

The specifics of the actual statistical logarithms can be challenged and argued among the academics. It is the key point that is critical. Please read carefully; there are many documented studies on the statistical quantifiable relationship between the work environment, and the productivity of the employees.[27]

Is it worth working toward a better social environment, especially when dealing with Gen X Managers and Employees, to gain a 4% increase in productivity? A 5% or 6% increase? Let's not argue the specific percentages. We are just not smart enough to understand the nuances of the variables. But do you get the point?

It will not happen without specific communication vehicles.

Vehicles: What do we need?

Management Support

This is perhaps the most critical element in the vehicles for motivating Gen Xers. I cannot emphasize it enough. I am talking about a major shift in corporate culture, in almost all of the corporations in America today.

That is why I started the book talking about the dynamics of an outside catalyst. *Companies are not going to change without a dynamic catalyst for change.* And whether the issues with Gen X or the shrinking employee pool are dynamic enough to get it done remains to be seen. Maybe it just will not happen in all companies, and if that is the case, then the reputation and ugly connotations regarding Gen X Managers will only increase in the years ahead. And that is sad.

But I can tell you that in some cases, it is happening now. And even going back to 1992, *Inc Magazine* reported that 30 CEOs of the *Inc 500* were age 30 or younger.[28] And in most cases, they get it. And for those of you who do not get it, guess what? Many of these companies are your competitors, and they are already changing the internal cultures of their work environment.

Almost every business journal or publication in America today is discussing a new area of corporate management. *"Human Capital Management"* no longer refers to *"reductions in labor expenses"* due to supposed increased efficiencies or technology. We have beaten that horse to death. But rather, "human capital management" refers to new creative customized employee programs geared to *increasing productivity.*

And not only are you competing against these companies with new management styles in the marketplace for customers, you are also competing for a pool of quality employees that for a 20-year window may be dramatically less than the pool you have available today. Wake up, corporate America.

I want to keep going, but I need to pause here to discuss an interesting phenomenon found in many businesses. It does not make any sense to me, but you decide for yourself.

In many corporations, managers are so frustrated by the high turnover ratio that they decide to acquiesce to high turnover as a constant in the equation of running a business. They have conceded that high turnover is a fact of life (remember the term McJob?) and they believe that investing in training for people, who are going to leave regardless, just does not make fiscal sense. Are you kidding me? *Please* do not give up on your employee's potential.

I can only shake my head. Training is critical; if we want to succeed we need for employees to understand the importance of their roles in the business. And what better way to demonstrate this to them then to invest in their futures. How about the needs of the Gen Xer?

Author Leonard L. Berry in his book *Discovering the Soul of Service* offers these comments, "Great service companies invest in employee success... Many firms, tormented by high employee turnover, avoid investing in employees because of their propensity to leave. The sample companies take the opposite approach, investing in the infrastructure, tools, and incentives necessary for employees' success."[29]

If this cultural adaptation is simply a patronization effort on the part of the Old School Managers then you are better off without it. And although it saddens me to write it, I believe that. Because in the traditional Old School style at least you have truth, and the patronization violates that truth. And truth is critical.

Unfortunately, we also need to get the Wanna-Bes on board. And if they think this shift in culture is purely a fad, they won't buy it, and I guarantee their employees will not buy into it either. It is not about political posturing; it is about real life. And to reach Gen X and Millennials, you are going to need more truth in management. Face it: They are too smart to be fooled. And they do not have enough trust to be swept into a pre-existing old school culture just because you say that it is the way we have always done it.

The Analytical Managers will want to wait, quantify, and will need to see the results from others, but by then it may be too late. And for the New Wavers, if your company does not want to shift its cultures to meet the needs of the future, then consider a change. Consider either a change in companies, or a change in careers. I do not make this recommendation lightly.

But the struggle you will face in your heart will tear you apart and lead to dishonesty. You cannot fool your Gen

X Managers. And although you may be good at fooling yourself, it will either change you, or kill you in the long run. I know, because I have been there. And I lived the results.

It may not be as bad for you as it was for me because I am an ENFP (Myers-Briggs Type Indicator ®). And in testing my personality profile, my "Feeling" side was off the chart. I was corporately trained to make decisions based on analysis and unfortunately I was very good at it. But my conflicting personality results indicated I needed to make decisions based on feelings not analysis. This scenario created an internal conflict so significant in me that it led to a mid-life melt down and chased me out of corporate management. There are many vehicles for identifying your "true self" and I encourage you to learn more about yourself at every opportunity.

I will demonstrate that vehicles do not need to be expensive, nor do they need to alienate management, even traditional management. In the next chapter I am going to talk about the Kaizen program. And if it works in the conservative business culture of a Japanese company, then the elements of the vehicle, not necessarily the program itself, will work for you too.

Remember, management support means 100% support from the top down. And that includes the CEO, the CFO, and often times the board. Get off the throne and into the game; the new game. You can do it; I believe in you.

But vehicles like Kaizen programs require the support of management, and in the Japanese management culture, they have 100% support. If I have not made my case by now, or if you still do not see the forest, then return the book to me for a refund. Or compete against us. Good luck. I hope your bench strength and your stable of young managers holds out in the years ahead. You do consider bench strength, don't you?

Budget – It doesn't need to be expensive

The beautiful thing about this shift in the corporate paradigms is that it does not need to be expensive. The answers are not found in expensive consultants (present company excluded of course) but in your existing employee base. After all, who knows more about the needs of the customer than those who talk to them every day? Who knows more about the tasks on the assembly line than those who work it every day?

But the communication will not just suddenly appear; there has to be a vehicle. Put the vehicles in place, and then let the Gen Xers establish their own programs to increase communication, morale, retention, and ultimately, productivity.

Yes, I am suggesting that you already have the creativity factor in house. You do not need to buy what you already own. And the fact that by involving the Gen Xer in the process provides equity, and equity improves retention, it all works. Want to get a promising Gen Xer involved in the growth of the company? Then put him or her on a task force to brainstorm ideas for strategic planning. Then, and this is critical, have them do a power point presentation to you on their findings. This demonstrates your truthful sincerity in the credibility of their opinions.

Remember, regardless of your true impression of the ideas, you must shower them with positive reinforcement. At the very least we have established equity and possibly uncovered a fresh new idea in the process. If you say you have tried that before, and it has not worked, you are committing murder and killing the vehicle. Instead say, "That is a good idea, we have tried some of that before, and here were the issues. What do you suggest?"

Every question should be responded to with "That's a good question"; giving positive reinforcement for asking and caring. Or, would you rather they just go to work brain dead until they leave and go to a competitor with more internal open vehicles for communication? These are the needs of the Gen Xer. And the cost of these ideas, well, the cost is minimal.

Positive Reinforcement

As we move forward I will suggest other templates for your review. Positive reinforcement is an essential element, because if it is not this idea that helps the corporation, it may be the next idea.

And without a vehicle and without positive reinforcement, you will never get to hear the second idea, or third. And even more importantly, the Gen Xer will never see the second opportunity, and if history is any indication, they will just leave and go to another company, and the spiral continues.

For you psychology majors, how do they get the rat to spin the miniature Ferris Wheel? They give the rat sugar water. But many managers trained in the art of intimidation, scare tactics and negative reinforcement, just don't get it. Or maybe you just do not have the patience or inclination to modify your management techniques. When was the last time you saw a research scientist standing in front of the rat cage, screaming at the rat? Many of you have been rewarding your salespeople with the rat technique for years, no pun intended. I, too, am a salesperson.

In the book *Whale Done* authors, Ken Blanchard, Thad Lacinak, Chuck Tompkins and Jim Ballard draw a parallel between positive reinforcement in management techniques and trust in the training of Shamu, the most dangerous predator in the ocean. Read it, because it makes sense.[30] Sound interesting? Familiar?

Historically, managers have acted only when the situation requires action. The old adage "if it ain't broke, don't fix it" no longer applies. The management gurus are all preaching from the same new hymnal.

Change your behavior, and get active when things are going well. Read that again. If you want to modify behavior, then practice sincere positive reinforcement every hour of every day with your staff. This is especially true when you are attempting to shift a cultural paradigm.

The words have to be honest and sincere. Remember the X-ray glasses in regard to false bravado. Also be aware that the majority of your message is sent through body language and tone of voice, so be honest in every aspect of your communication.

100% Participation

I want to stay on the characteristics of successful vehicles, especially as they apply to motivation, communication and retention for Gen X Managers and Employees, but I have to mention how Stephen R. Covey's *The 7 Habits of Highly Effective People*[31] has dramatically influenced my opinions on management techniques.

From the time we wore corporate diapers, we have heard stories about the great Horatio Alger in the business world. We were raised to admire those who were independent, to respect those who were "self-made men".

Admit it: "We were raised to stand on our own two feet". In our business world, total independence has often been the ultimate goal, the benchmark for success. Individual leadership techniques, individual profit centers, incentive contests with the biggest prize going to the single winner. We even purchased divisions and companies to be vertically integrated; we then went out and shopped other competitors for the best individual deals.

Covey introduced me to this concept. I knew it existed, the level above independence, the level of "interdependence." He talks about a Win/Win scenario. Win/Win is a frame of mind and heart that constantly seeks mutual benefit in all human interactions. Win/Win means that agreements or solutions are mutually beneficial, mutually satisfying. With a Win/Win solution, all parties feel good about the decision and feel committed to the action plan. Win/Win sees life as a cooperative, not a competitive arena. It's not your way, or my way; it's a better way, a higher way."[32]

Traditionally in American business, we have considered an incentive program to be a contest of sorts. The misguided goal was to be the "Best Salesperson", or more pathetically the "Employee of the Year". I cringe every time I see a picture on the wall, or worse yet, a parking place designation, usually strategically placed where every visitor/customer needs to walk around the car or truck just to get in the front door of your business. I think I am going to be sick.

Programs that single out individual performance should be boxed up and sent to a museum and displayed next to the petrified dinosaur dung collection. I told you I was going to trash the concept, so stay tuned.

These types of contests are counterproductive. First, can we agree that an effective team is better than an effective individual? Can you rely on one or two individuals to carry your entire organization? Then why would you create individualistic incentives that encourage individual versus team behavior? I just do not get it, and I am a Boomer.

The Gen Xer will see individual programs as another corporate version of the Miss America Pageant. No offense to Miss America, and I hope none taken. The Japanese get it, and it took a while before I accepted it too. Especially in managing sales people, but I was wrong.

Participation must be across the board, inclusive, period. Now, that is not to say that individuals should not be recognized for outstanding achievement, but I will take a Super Bowl Championship over the individual quarterback with the highest rating or the most passing yards, every day of the week. And if you ask the quarterbacks, they would agree. Do you get this analogy?

And by the way, before I exit the proverbial soapbox, 100% participation does not mean for all those under the throne. The king or queen has to be in this deal too. I am sorry, I am trying to let it go, but I just can't. The 100% participation element is so critical to dealing with the next generation of employees, I just have to write one more metaphor.

Many of the emotional elements we are discussing are not unique to Gen Xers, who just react differently than we were taught to react. Emotions are universal, although our business schools historically have done a good job of taking them out of our management technique toolbox. Now who is aloof? But I digress again.

Did you ever join a Little League team and not get to play? Ever sat on the bench waiting for an opportunity that never came? Have you ever been cut from a team, or not selected for a work group or committee? *Have you ever had a daughter who did not get asked to the prom?* Let me tell you it is an awful, helpless feeling. And although the example may be a metaphor, the feelings of alienation and pain are real.

Abbey Story, Participation

A few years ago I watched my daughter, a back-up point guard at the time, sit on the bench during a middle school championship basketball game. Now, Abbey had skills, she had led the point on championship teams in the past. But this team lost this game, and Abbey never had a chance to play. The starters were exhausted and lost a lead, and ultimately lost the game in the final minutes. As long as I live, I will never forget the long ride home.

This is not a metaphor about the attributes of coaching, or maybe it is. Abbey is a great athlete and the consummate team player. But that night was the last time she ever competitively walked on a basketball court, and that is sad. I helplessly held her in my arms as she cried lonely tears. What could I say?

All she wanted was a chance to play. All of the good things that had happened over the previous two months, the breakaways, the steals, the victories, the laughing, the come-from-behind victories, the team sleepovers and the awesome feeling of being a member of a team were gone. Two months of happiness and hard work vanished as an old game clock slowly clicked down at the far end of the gym.

I cherish the time I spend coaching youth lacrosse. And I empathize with the dilemma all coaches and managers go through. And from that painful evening, I learned to be a better coach. At the beginning of the season, we talk about participation and teamwork. And we explain to our starters that we will play all of the players because their involvement is critical to the success of the team. This type of open communication and honesty is critical to the success of the program.

At the high school level, we do our substituting early in the game; we get the entire team active in the process, as early as the first few minutes of the first half. Everyone plays, and everyone supports the players on the field. Remember, positive reinforcement across the board. In the end, we play to win, with the best players, and the enthusiasm from the entire bench is awesome.

The point is, with a little imagination, managers can make everyone feel involved, and still play to win. And that is your challenge. Do you remember the lonely feelings we discussed, the feelings of being an outsider on your own team? Now transfer the feelings of a parent in that scenario to managing your own Gen X Employees. Creativity is not expensive.

Now, with that off my chest, we can move on. And incidentally, in case you were wondering, Abbey went on to become an MVP volleyball player. She is a player who cheers and supports members of her team regardless of their talent. She and I will both never forget that day. And I am so proud of her.

Empowerment

Is this a big word or what? When you hear senior executives in America today talk about Employee Empowerment, it is like a 66-pound Cheshire cat choking on a fur ball. Employee Empowerment scares the hell out of the Old Schoolers and sends Wanna-Bes and Analyticals scrambling to the men's room for solitude faster than rabid dogs on a piece of red meat. Why doesn't anyone want to talk about empowerment?

Oh sure, a senior level manager recently told me he is all for empowerment, but employees want the power without the accountability. And although he was tossing out buzzwords, there is an ounce of truth in his five pounds of self-rationalization.

Why can't we talk about the value of empowerment without managers freaking out about their perceived lack of control? Can you say P-O-W-E-R? Let's go back to the dialogue about Employee Equity; is there really that much of a major difference between the two concepts?

Last I checked the Ritz-Carlton Hotels in Atlanta are still standing. The Ritz-Carlton Group, also known as the poster child for empowerment, is surviving. Things have changed, and I will grant you that.

Can you imagine the risk of granting every employee the ability to authorize up to $ 2,000 per day to make a guest happy? Talk about your clean towels. What are the chances of that happening in your company? But at the next level, *can you imagine how the employees felt with this kind of power?* Now substitute the word "trust" for the word "power". It had to have been amazing"– scary yes – but amazing nonetheless.

OK, so this $ 2,000 a day example is the prime rib of empowerment. Where does it say that your company cannot start with a little cutlet here and there? If we get the employees active in the process and provide them the vehicles they need to be heard, it is a natural progression to give them empowerment as well.

It is like being half pregnant, not that I would know. Otherwise the result is construed as negative reinforcement. The weak will go back into their brainless day-to-day existence in the office, and the strong, well, they will just find another job. After all, they are all aloof, as you know.

And accountability is important. But not the way you may think. It is not a case of paying a price for a mistake. *That is not accountability at all; that is punishment. And most managers do not understand the difference.* We are not talking about a payroll deduction plan from their meager weekly allowance.

I submit to you that a better vehicle for accountability is for the group to do an honest follow-up analysis, or a review. Give them some credit. *Remember, you do not have to lead the horse to water. You just need to tell the horse why water is important.* One battle does not win or lose a war.

And often times the mistakes will ultimately result in long-term success. Go back to *your* management mirror, did you learn from the *mistakes in your career?*

Chapter 16

Kaizen

Kaizen

*Kaizens are continuous improvements made by employees to improve a process or equipment.

*A Kaizen can be implemented by an individual or a group.

I n my eight years at Yamaha Motor Manufacturing Corporation I was exposed to many of the inherent elements of the Japanese business culture, including many things I would have never seen by working in domestic organizations.

I learned about decisions by committee, I learned about consensus before action. I learned about a new value of time. For the Japanese, manufacturing and distributing a product for 25 years is still considered in the start-up mode. I learned about the 5-S program, photos on the outside of cabinets, and the office police. The most powerful of all of these programs, and perhaps the cornerstone in manufacturing, was the Kaizen program.

Suffice it to say that Kaizen translates to "improvement". But in this environment the concept went far beyond an employee program, far beyond a quality circle, and far beyond even the term culture. It is a way of life, a living process.

On my first tour of the new Yamaha factory, I was inundated with the Kaizen program. To begin, the first thing that the employees see when they enter the building is the Kaizen Board. As you walk through the factory, every 20 feet or so, you see a reference to the Kaizen achievements of each department, Kaizens for assembly, Kaizens for paint, and so on. The references are banners, or giant posters, or stand-up educational instruction sheets for each individual section of the manufacturing process.

My intent here is not to convince you to implement a Kaizen process in your place of business, although you could do worse things. My intent is to demonstrate the parallels between the Kaizen process and the vehicles we discussed in Chapter 15. This program is used purely as an example or even a metaphor for what you can accomplish with the appropriate vehicles.

The Kaizen process begins when an employee sees something in his job that needs to be improved. It does not sound complicated, because it is not. It may be as simple as a leaking pipe, or unsafe clearance for those walking through. Or it may be as complex as modifying techniques for adhesives, paint lines or quality control. The employee then fills out a Kaizen sheet, or form.

The form is not complicated either. It can be typed, or often just filled out by hand. The written sections of the form are supplemented or enhanced by open spaces designated for pictures. The employee provides a description of the problem, as well as a Polaroid photo of the current situation. Then the employee briefly states the recommended corrective action and then provides a picture when the idea is put into implementation.

The implemented idea on the form is then submitted to a committee made up of peers for their approval. Notice I said peers, not management. After a short period of time for testing, the committee meets to decide whether or not to keep the suggested improvement as a standard part of the process. Not too complicated, eh?

The employee is rewarded with a bronze pin for his or her employee security badge. Ah, now we have status and recognition. There are three levels of colors for the pins. For example, after five suggestions, the bronze pin is replaced with a silver pin, and following the next level of ideas submitted, ultimately a gold pin.

It is interesting to note that the *significance* of the suggestion is not recognized with the positive reinforcement of the status-laden pin, but the rewards are for the employees participating in the process. You may want to read that sentence again.

The process is then expanded to the number of suggestions submitted by the people who work in the same group, then the same department, then recognized across the facility as a whole. As a matter of fact, the Kaizen Board I mentioned previously displays all of the current Kaizens, listed by department, for all of the employees to see.

Talk about peer pressure management. At this point I would like to ask the Analyticals, "What do you think the cost of that small pin is versus the perceived value from the peer group?"

There are also supplemental incentives. Every quarter, all who have submitted suggestions are eligible for a drawing for great prizes. Prizes are not for the best idea mind you, but for the employees' participation in the process. And, at the end of the year, a select group of those departments, (usually for Kaizens submitted as a group activity), are invited in front of the Executive Committee for a Power Point presentation on their specific Kaizen improvements.

The winning team is then sent to present its Kaizen presentation at a Yamaha factory abroad. While I was on the executive team, we sent the winning group to a Yamaha plant in France.

And equally as important, they reported about their trip upon their return. It works, can you see why? The vehicle is in place. I told you this chapter is really not about selling the Kaizen program, but is to be used as a metaphor.

With a little creativity, and a little equity, with empowerment – don't gag – the same types of programs can be implemented into your culture as well. Do not freak out if the answers are not at your fingertips. I will bet the answers lie within *your* employee pool too.

The program itself is not the critical concept here. The important concept is how it improves the overall business and gives the employees equity in the process at the same time. It even works with Gen Xers; you will see. But you have to have a vehicle.

Does the vehicle meet the criteria?

Management Support

The program is really not a program at all, but instead a way of life, a process. Included in the daily peer review of the large Kaizen Board are all of the managers as well. Middle managers are always encouraging their groups to take the time and submit even more Kaizens.

Moreover, when important senior level managers visit from Japan, they are also included in the Kaizen presentations. Can you imagine the power an hourly employee feels when presenting in front of a board member from Japan, complete with an interpreter? Or even in front of the factory's Executive Committee?

This particular vehicle has the total support of all those in management.

Budget

As you can see, this is not an expensive program. Kaizens meet the parameters for small budgets used on effective vehicles. It is not unusual for vendors to assist in donating prizes for the quarterly drawings. Based on more than 1,000 employees, the cost is insignificant in terms of the overall budget. Pins and paper, even we can afford that.

Positive Reinforcement

The reinforcement is not only demonstrated by management, but also by the individual teams, and the total group of peers. The pins are far more significant than even a check would be, as they accomplish so much more, and are worn daily.

100% Participation

The Kaizen program clearly meets the participation criteria, from small groups to the entire worker population. As a matter of fact, the dates of hire are also on the badges, and peer pressure dictates that one does not want to have been an employee for three or four years without a Kaizen pin. That peer pressure management, albeit in a subtle fashion, works again.

Empowerment

Without the inputs from the Kaizen process I am confident that the plant would not have had the high efficiency ratings. Ideas were submitted, and ideas were implemented, on a daily or weekly basis. And this empowerment program did not break the bank. So put the hairball back in your throat.

The interesting paradox here is that I have been talking about *progressive shifts in management cultures to accommodate the unique characteristics of the Gen X Managers and Employees.* The inherent connotation is for a new style of management.

The irony lies in the fact that the Japanese management is extremely conservative and extremely slow to change. And this program has been in existence for decades.

This is not a commentary on Japanese business culture, just an interesting observation. Maybe it is true that there is nothing new under the sun, but what does that say about us, and our ability to find ways to retain Gen X Managers?

Chapter 17

The QBM

The QBM is a vehicle I developed with the help of others in the management team when I was a vice-president with North Coast Distributing, in Cleveland, Ohio. The program was designed to enhance communication and develop employee equity. The program was written under a fun social format, but the communication and teambuilding results were amazing. I cannot take the credit; it was the employees who took the program and ran with the concept. And I thank them every time I present it to a new client.

This program was designed to meet the needs of a smaller company, 30 to 100 employees. In companies of this size, specific vehicles for training, communication, and teambuilding are the first to be cut in the budget editing room. I am not making a judgment, just restating a fact of small business.

The program requires a meeting place, preferably on site, to accommodate the vehicle. This can be done in a large meeting room, as we used, or even a small lunchroom. But on site works best, and I will get to that.

The Quarterly Business Meeting

At the time, North Coast was in a period of rapid growth. The company was small – 60 employees or so – but had different departments: Parts, Commercial Product Sales, Consumer Product Sales, Irrigation Product Sales Service, Warehouse/Transportation, and Administration, including Accounting. There was new ownership, and well, we all know the anxieties of new ownership.

The idea was to have a small theme-oriented meeting/party once every three months, each hosted by a different department. The themes were the responsibility of the host department. The ideas were creative: Christmas in July, Mexican, Pajama Party, Wine Tasting, Beach Party and so on. You get the idea. The critical purpose of themes is to make it an event...not just another meeting.

The meetings were held on a Friday afternoon, beginning a 4:00 p.m., and usually ran to 6:00 p.m. or 6:30 p.m. And, they were on the clock. Don't freak; the total budget given to the host department was $250 per meeting, although in today's market it might need to be $300. Not much, when compared to the results. *The low budget forces the hosts to be resourceful and creative.* Stay with me.

The party theme aspect of this vehicle is critical, as it acts as an icebreaker and also has a tendency to break down any of the subtle or not so subtle communication "walls" built during the previous quarter. For example, issues between sales and accounting, or commercial products and service on equipment. But then again, you probably don't have those. It is tough to maintain an attitude toward someone in Accounting when they are wearing a pajama top, or a sombrero.

I understand that these little scraps between departments were geographically unique to Ohio-based companies, and if you are located somewhere else in the country, then by definition, you just do not have these types of issues in your companies. But let me continue anyway.

The reason the program works best if conducted on site is the need for creative decorations, as they set the mood. If you do not have a lunchroom, or conference room, try a section of the warehouse. Creativity is key. The department setting up the room for the QBM decides on the decorations, and decorates the room. And unofficially, now we have a unique teambuilding activity. Are you still with me?

Often times I felt as though I was entering a small gymnasium for a prom. The Beach parties had sand boxes and sand castles, Christmas in July, well everyone likes Christmas. Mexican came complete with tacos and pinatas. Members of the host department started at noon on Friday to begin the decorating and other preparations. Thus, on site is best.

The theme was carried through the appetizers and food selections. These items could be purchased but often times they were made at home by members of the host department. These were all done under the cloak of surprise for all of the others attending, until a few days before the meeting. Creating the theme, decorations and food, and keeping it a departmental secret contributed toward the fun. The peer pressure to "one up" the previous QBM made the employees even more dedicated toward pulling off a great meeting.

All employees are directed to participate in the theme. The hosts need to have some extra small items to attach to those who think they are too important to participate. Or, the host group may want to provide an item representing the theme for everyone in attendance.

The beautiful thing here is that management is a non-player in the entire process except for two small responsibilities. First, management has to sincerely encourage everyone to participate. And secondly, it is critical that senior management actively participate in the theme. If you do not participate, then the Wanna-Bes are definitely not going to participate.

You can do this without embarrassing yourself. Be creative, even if it is a quiet creative. You do remember how to do that, don't you? It can be as simple as wearing a cap over your Brooks Brothers suit. I am telling you it is critical, and if you cannot bring yourself to do these two little things, then you might just forget about the program for your company, and read on for amusement purposes only.

For those senior managers who fit the "Themes are OK for them, but not OK for me" stereotype, I might suggest buying thick curtains for your corner office windows, so you do not have to watch the exodus of Gen X Managers and Employees from your parking lot. Now that that's off my chest, let's continue.

Even middle managers are excluded from planning or presentations. It forces the employees to work together and participate, not because management will slap them on the wrist, but because they are under the analytical spotlight of their peers.

After 15 or 20 minutes of social time, the meeting begins. An hourly employee representing the host department does the welcome speech (3-5 minutes) and announces the agenda of speakers. At this point, an hourly non-manager, gets up from each group or department and has eight to 10 minutes to bring all of the other employees up to speed on what has happened in his or her department over the past three months, and what the department's plans are to improve the business over the next three months.

It was amazing what I learned through those presentations, but more importantly what all the employees learned as well. The presentations were honest to a fault and included the good things as well as the not-so-good things. I remember the audience cheering when the sales team announced a new deal and booing when the sales team announced it had lost the sale on a new golf project.

They were not booing at the sales team; they were booing at the customer for not making the right decision, at least in their eyes. But then again, remember, many of them were in robes or pajamas, so consider the source. I meant to say the employees were in robes; most of our customers wore more traditional clothing.

The administrative representatives would be frank about problems and frustrations with computer conversions; the parts staff discussed wrestling with fill rates. It was honest, and remember, through honesty stems trust. And trust is critical.

Speaking of honesty, a selected representative from Accounting – not the CFO or owner, (remember the Gen Xer will not trust them!) – would speak on the quarterly financials. I recommend putting this presentation in the middle of the other speakers, as this meeting is not designed to concentrate on numbers. There is a time and a place for everything.

In order to prepare to speak for the 10-minute presentation, the designated representative, never the same person, would actually have to go and talk to each member of his department for input. I believe one of the key elements was the verbal communication. The idea here is to establish people-to-people communication so please do not use forms or emails. Presentations often included engagements or graduations and were cheered by the audience.

After a year or so, the whole thing goes to the next level. I saw presentations delivered as teams of rappers using rap lyrics, and I saw presentations filmed and mixed on home video cameras. *But then again, maybe you do not want to see this type of creativity among your different departments, or honesty in communication.*

The vehicle of a QBM takes empowerment to be successful, but it will not break the bank. And remember, if you are adventurous enough to try this at home, (metaphor silly), every effort needs to be rewarded with positive reinforcement. The management support required is not direct active involvement but rather support of the process, and the minimal time and financial investments required.

Your first QBM may be a little stilted; but remember, just tell the horse, and the horse will take care of the rest. It may take two or three meetings to get it going, but have faith in your employees, and support them with positive comments.

One role that management may serve in this process is the prompting of applause or cheering on each good item reported. I do not know why, but if the boss cheers or whistles, it just loosens everyone up, and this is designed to be an upbeat meeting. I can tell you from my experience at North Coast, and at others that have implemented this program, the employees look forward to the meetings with a passion. Isn't that a switch?

One of my clients in Florida actually opens QBMs by inviting a customer to briefly speak about his or her company to open the meeting. Not only is it a great idea, but, it came from the employees; that speaks to their equity in the process. Can you imagine the equity that is felt by the customer in the relationship? What if the customer representative is Gen X? Pretty cool.

I get asked the question about changing the timing to monthly QBM's. I may be wrong or jaded by my own positive experiences, but once a quarter seems to work better. The meetings are far enough apart to create anticipation, and it makes each QBM seem like an event instead of a regular activity.

So what do we have at the end of the day? We have an inexpensive program that is a dynamic vehicle for communication within even a small organization. We have many unique training parallels between the business and the QBM.

Listen carefully: The host group meets and develops the theme, meets and plans the food and decorations as well as the process to get the ideas implemented on time, then conducts the meeting. The rest of the employees follow the lead and dress according to the theme of the meeting. *We have creativity, equity, communication, education, and participation. Can you see the parallel between this type of activity and how you would like to see your departments operate, or cooperate?* Did it cost a lot of money? Based on what you know about Gen X, will this work? Why?

Yes, I know you have a company newsletter. It is OK, but it is an old institution. This, the QBM, is a great program in the appropriate application. It will generate communication, support and enthusiasm. It gets people involved in the culture of the organization and meets the established criteria for a strong vehicle. Can you say the same for your newsletter, if you were to compare the two options? Come on, are you kidding?

Chapter 18

W.O.S.

This next program works especially well in companies focusing on customer service, hospitality, or retail.

Although with a little input from your employees (equity), the WOS program can be modified to meet the needs of almost any organization.

I really borrowed the original concept from my friends at PGA West. I just expanded the idea to better address the needs of the Gen X Managers and Employees and to meet the established guidelines for vehicles in Chapter 15. You may also recognize some of the same characteristics from a "Mystery Shopper" campaign.

Anyway, a few years ago, I was asked to say a few words at the regularly scheduled meeting of the management team at PGA West. And I want to thank my friend

Joey Garon for the invitation, as well as the concept for the original idea. I guess there were about 30 managers in attendance representing eight or so resort golf properties in La Quinta, Palm Springs, California.

As part of the normal agenda for the management meeting, a selected manager was chosen to conduct his own private tour of an individual resort facility in the KSL network and report to the group on his observations. The process was very serious, especially for Joey. I was kind of surprised. You would be, too, if you knew Joey Garon. He is perhaps one of the best general managers in the country, but he marches to a different drummer, probably more like a giddy tambourine player with a Heineken in one hand.

The comments ranged from the appearance of the entry to recognizing the critical nature of first impressions (more on that later) to length of lines at the retail counters. The comments also ranged from observations of trash in the flowerbeds (although they looked pretty amazing to me) to potential safety concerns due to small construction projects. The tours were comprehensive, from the front door to the back door, and all rest rooms between.

Weekly Observation Sheets

I was impressed with the depth of the analysis, but that little voice was ringing again. In this case, I think everyone who attended learned something; I know I did. Managers were writing notes, smiling, and discussing the pros and cons of different solutions, all in an open atmosphere. The voice in my head was telling me to go beyond.

Since that day, I have recommended and seen clients put this idea into action. We just modified the idea, made the program more comprehensive for all employees and simplified the process at the same time.

We start with a florescent-colored piece of standard notebook-sized paper that we cut in half after printing. On the top of the form is the name of the facility and logo to make it official; no seriously, official is good. The form contains a place for the name of the employee, the date, and two options.

Mx Marketing
Weekly Observation Sheet

Date: _____

Name: _____

We did it Right! ...

_____

_____

_____

We need to improve ...

_____

_____

_____

The first option is to state briefly something that the employee noticed during the month the organization, or if done by department, the department was doing right. Remember, it is OK to accentuate the positive. That is why I have the positive option listed first on the form. It may be a comment from a customer thanking them for the service, or answering a question quickly and efficiently. It may be a disaster averted, or a cold bottled water for a waiting customer.

The second option is a space or line that gives the employee an opportunity to note a comment on something that the organization or the department needs to improve. It may be as simple as answering the telephone without letting it ring 20 times. Don't you hate that? Or better signage to assist new visitors, or information pamphlets. Get it?

The employee is required to fill out only one of the spaces. He does not need to note both a positive and an opportunity to improve, just one or the other. The result is a program initiated by management, yet a program that gives the employee choices, just like a grownup.

Key Components

I recommend that this be done on a monthly basis to keep it from getting old, although I have some clients running the program twice a month. Secondly, now listen closely; it is important that this program be introduced to new employees as part of the orientation process, but I will write more on that later. It is also imperative that all employees fill out the forms every month, no discussion, and no excuses. 100% participation.

The third critical aspect is the follow-up meeting. This is another good reason to do this monthly. The employees gather in a relaxed setting with the department head or a manager to review the responses. Those that require an action plan to improve are sent to a small, three or four-member task force for ideas on how they can be improved, and implemented.

The task force, or the "Answer Team", does not include a manager, but does include the employee with the suggestion. Equity and Empowerment, and how much did this program cost?

Management demonstrates its support by verbally, or in some cases via email, thanking the employees for their responses, with select examples on how the implemented ideas have improved the overall operation.

If the program is introduced in a larger company, once every six months, one of the Answer Teams rotates to other departments, and they present a quick synopsis of some of the reported observations, selecting three positive attributes or experiences as well as three improvements.

Can you imagine the bump in attitude of Gen Xers when his ideas are presented, or when he gets the opportunity to present to a neighboring department? It is awesome. Yes, this program is also a derivative of the Kaizen program.

And again, the program meets the criteria of a strong vehicle; management support, low budget, positive reinforcement from the peer level, 100% participation, and employee empowerment. And managers can do what they do best: strategically manage the business and let the employees concentrate on their individual areas of responsibility. It keeps them active, gives them equity, and frankly, they know more about the grass root activity than you do. Sorry, but that is the truth, so let it go.

Chapter 19

Mentoring / Employee Exchange Programs

I am going to discuss these two concepts in the same chapter due to their similarities and objectives. The unique aspect of these two programs is their ability to meet simultaneously two important needs of Gen Xers. Not only do they satisfy the need for equity in the new or existing employees, but they also meet the same need of equity in the sponsoring employee or group. Don't get confused; I may have made it more complicated than it really is, and I will explain.

Mentoring /Ambassador

The mentoring program is designed for new hires to an organization. The first objective is to make the new employee feel more comfortable, and give him a friendly conduit to express concerns or questions. Would you agree that all positions in an organization have a learning curve? I would submit there are actually two learning curves. And can we all agree that the sooner employees get up to speed, the sooner they can be effective?

There is a learning curve on the pure objective details of the specific job function. And secondly, there is a curve on learning the unique characteristics of each organization. And I am going to let it go at that. Managers seem to concentrate on the first, or at the very least, managers seem to get the two confused. Mentoring helps on both fronts. The mentoring program continues, once a week for the first month of employment for the new hire. Implementing this program for just the first month seems to work best.

If you like the term mentoring, I can live with that. Another name for this important function may be an "Ambassador". I just like the connotation of "ambassador". The implication is more of a selected representative rather than of a babysitter.

Once a week, either at the beginning of the week or as I would recommend at the end of the week, the new employee meets with the ambassador to discuss the activities of the week. The end of the week works better to give the opportunity for the new hire to end the week on a positive note. All issues are better when identified sooner rather than later.

You can already see where this dialogue might be negative or dangerous, but read on with an open mind, and do not sell your employees short. We can address your concerns with a short training session for those who will act as mentors or ambassadors. Actually, it is not always the same person, and so it may be a few sessions.

In this meeting, the mentor asks open questions about the activities of the week, and then listens. A good example would be, "Please tell me a little bit about how you felt at work this week." Then the ambassador has to close up and listen for the response.

Questions from the employees usually range from parking lot options to more personal questions such as, "Is Joe really such a jerk?" That is where the mentor training comes into play. The mentor is trained as an ambassador for the company and must be selected with this in mind. Training for the ambassador should include communication skills on listening, as well as body language and tone of voice.

And every response from the mentor should include "good question", as it will make the new hire feel not only more comfortable asking questions, but also more important. In most cases the new hire is Gen X and reinforcing questions will just play to the natural characteristics of the new hire.

There are two schools of thought on selecting the ambassador best suited for the new hire. You have the option of selecting someone of similar age, gender or position, or of throwing caution to the wind and mixing Gen Xers with Boomers right from the get go. My recommendation may surprise you, and although I see the merits of the first option, I like to mix it up a little.

The purpose of the program is to make the employee feel welcome and shorten up the learning curves, especially the second curve. The program is not designed to be a vehicle that introduces a new best friend. In this case, different frames of reference are better, I believe. It begins to set the stage for Boomers and Gen Xers to work together.

At the beginning of this section, I told you there were a number of objectives. Equally important are the needs satisfied in the selection of the mentor. Everyone was new to the company at one time or another, and in the case of

Gen Xers, I guess a little more often than the norm.

By giving the mentor/ambassador the responsibility of lessening the learning curve for the new hire, management is placing trust in the mentor. Remember trust builds loyalty and so on. I believe everyone recognizes that the sooner the new hire is up to speed, the better for the corporation, and this important responsibility is being turned over to the mentor.

This program satisfies the needs of Gen Xers on both sides of the table. Management support is demonstrated through trust. It, again, does not require a large budget. It incorporates positive reinforcement, 100% participation in new hires, equity and empowerment.

Tailoring programs to include vehicles to meet the needs of Gen Xers is not as tough as you thought. Incidentally, you may also want to try a version of this program in small groups instead of one on one. Both ideas have merit.

Trust your employees. You are still the manager, but empowering employees and demonstrating equity will make your company stronger. I am not asking you to give up your power or position, just to modify your techniques and programs. They are your future.

Employee Exchange Programs

If your organization has just gone through a merger or acquisition, please consider this program sooner rather than later. It will save you headaches down the road and open lines of communication immediately. Although I promise you the program will provide great results in any situation.

To be honest, this one was not my idea either. Are you seeing a pattern here? I first saw a version of this idea in use in the golf industry, with Club Corporation of America. In case you are not familiar with CCA, they are one of the largest national accounts in the golf industry. They are also an organization that historically has been good with employee programs and training.

Even the golf industry is made of segments. Outside, a Golf Course Superintendent, golf operations and pro shop often run by a Golf Professional, while an F&B Manager or a General Manager manages the food and beverage operations. In some cases all three report to the board or owner, and in some cases all functions report to the General Manager. In the golf industry there is also an unwritten rule that all three segments remain independent, and they should never work together for the common good. Why? Because that is the way we have always done it, that's why. Just kidding.

It is also critically important that they do not communicate to each other, have individualistic goals and objectives, have little or no respect for the functions of the other segments, and talk about each other as much as possible in the confines of the back room. Does this sound familiar to you? Is it your club? Just another metaphor in case you missed it: It is really not about clubs; it is about your business.

Anyway, during my membership time at Firestone Country Club, a CCA showcase facility, I enjoyed meeting and talking to many of the employees in all segments of the well-run facility. You may not know that I started my career 25 years ago in the golf industry shining shoes in the back room of Columbus Brookside C.C., so golf operations are near and dear to my heart. Actually, had I ever been smart enough to calibrate a sprayer; I may have been a golf course superintendent today. Instead, well, let's just move on.

One of the major differences between the new managers of tomorrow for the inside operations and those who work outside for the superintendent are not so much their personalities, but instead are thinner waistlines and the amount of hair gel that is applied to the hair on a daily, or hourly basis. Sorry. No offense was intended to those of you into hair gel.

One day, I was playing golf on the South Course and approached a work crew edging bunkers. Edging bunkers at a golf course in the summer is one of the worst activities you could ever imagine. It was a job reserved for those who had tried to date the daughter of the superintendent.

Most work was done by hand in those days, and between the fire ants, yellow jackets, and incoming golf balls, it was a job not for the faint of heart. Throw in a little Midwest heat and humidity – well you get the point.

As I approached the bunker, I spotted one of the young gel-kings from inside the pro shop slaving away in the bunker. I asked him, "What is a nice guy like you doing working in a place like this?" Can you imagine the effect of the heat and humidity on his hair?

He responded that as a part of his training to be a General Manager in the CCA network, he was required to spend a portion of the summer working on the grounds crew. And from there, this twist on employee exchange programs was born.

How and Why

I love this program. It has a tendency to open a lot of eyes within the corporation, enhances communication and teamwork, and establishes equity. In many companies, different departments, although they are located in the same complex or even the same building, operate as though they were in different continents. If we can get 500 channels off of a satellite feed, why can't we get three different departments to act as one unified organization?

I know the answer; it is tied back to that independence issue. Individual visions, goals, compensation plans; where is interdependence when you need it? Will we ever change? I hope so.

The employee exchange program works best in larger corporations, but when scaled down, it can be an excellent vehicle in smaller companies as well. On the surface it may seem simple, but I can assure you that on a deeper level it is powerful for a number of reasons. In order to maximize the benefits, there are two distinct parts to the process. This first part is the exchange, the second part, the reporting after the exchange.

Once again, I like a monthly rotation for this process, but I have clients who prefer a quarterly rotation. This concept works with hourly workers as well as middle managers. The process begins when two managers choose two employees for the exchange program. I like to choose somebody with a meager attitude, or someone I would like to pick up a notch or two. It is not necessarily a reward for your best employee.

The two employees will work together for the period, for example, one week in one participant's position, then one week in the second participant's position. The downside may be you have to give up the employee for two days, or up to a week, although you can modify the time commitment. But remember one full day is an absolute minimum.

The selected employee is sent to work with a peer, in a different department or division, someone at the same level of management or pay scale for two days to a week. The session begins with a review of the current job descriptions, goals and current projects. These are outlined on a blank form supplied by management and filled out by the host manager or employee.

The form has spaces for job descriptions, goals, and current projects, and underneath are spaces for the following observations: Three things I expected to see, three things I was surprised to see, and the single most significant piece of information I learned. I could give you a better template form, but as you now know, that would not give you equity in the process. Stop complaining in your own mind and please just read on.

The host employee has the guest with him or her for the entire period. As an alternative, some have done this as a half-day project for five days in a row to accommodate real-life logistical situations. Following the first week, the process is repeated by reversing the host employee. This part of the session ends in a mutual discussion with both applicants filling out their respective forms together, and making copies for their counterparts, or exchange partners.

The second and perhaps more critical part of the vehicle is the follow-up meeting within the original department. I do not like these to be conducted over a lunch meeting for a host of reasons: It impedes on what the employee considers free time – there are too many distractions outside of the business – shall I keep listing reasons why not to do the follow up meeting over lunch, or do you get the point?

In order to get the most out of this experience, set up a formal meeting in the conference room or some other private area. It conveys importance. It symbolizes credibility, which helps build trust – you know the drill. The participant shares copies of both forms with the other members in the department.

The participant then verbally, or even via power point, reviews his observations with the rest of the group. As the senior manager, demonstrate your support by attending as many of these sessions as you can. No, you need to attend each session. Imagine the feeling of the participant if you blow off his or her session but attend somebody else's presentation. Remember Abbey, and the championship game ...

Mx Marketing, LLC

Employee Exchange Report

Date: _____

Host Department _____

Visiting Department _____

Name: _____

Job Description: _____

Goals: _____

_____

3 Things I Expected to Observe:

_____

_____

_____

3 Things I was Surprised to Observe:

_____

_____

_____

The biggest surprise from the exchange was….

_____

I want to consider implementing…

_____

Keep in mind the doubts of Gen Xers in regard to senior management. You are allowed to ask basic questions, but basically it is not your show, and this aspect is critical, so just nod your head and smile. If you are a Wanna-Be it will not be that difficult. Can you understand that? If it means rescheduling for all to attend, do it; we need your support.

The worst thing that can happen is the other manager or employees will learn something new about the day-to-day activities in another department. More often than not, both parties will have an eye-opening experience, and by the communication process with their peers, you will build the trust and equity in the presenters.

It is amazing how there will be obvious parallels in the issues facing the different departments. And often times by discussing the issues in an outside department, in the third person as it were, you will find new ideas that will help in your department as well. It is similar to a case study: Far enough away to lend objectivity but close enough to home to make it real.

Following the first exchange, do not be surprised if you have other managers or employees asking you to be the next participant. It is fun, it is effective, it is educational, and it is inexpensive. It is a great way to keep the Gen Xers in the game. If you traveled 10 years back in your career, and you were chosen to be the participant, how would you feel about yourself? Your company? Your manager?

In smaller companies, it seems as though almost everybody knows everybody anyway. But I would not hesitate to put a sales person in the parts department, or service, or receivables. Imagine that if you will, a salesperson in receivables. And the reverse would also be effective. But remember the vehicle without the follow-up meeting is only half a vehicle and will not work to establish trust and equity. You will gain knowledge and appreciation, but reporting back to the original peer group accomplishes so much more psychologically for the Gen Xer.

And finally, early in the book, I touched on the transient nature of the Gen Xer. It may be that if you have a good employee, this process may interest him or her in moving within your organization, instead of outside of your organization. This program works, and although it does not meet the total participation requirement for a strong vehicle, it is a proven performer in dealing with Gen X Managers, guaranteed.

Chapter 20

Interviewing / Orientation

A re we getting somewhere yet? In my on going discussions with you regarding Gen X Managers and Employees this is going to seem a little weird. And you thought that Gen Xers were aloof.

I decided to make one of the last chapters in the book about the *beginning* of the process for hiring Gen X. It is not the first time I have recommended turning a process or an organization upside down. But by now, I hope you see, that at least in my own mind there is a method behind the madness.

Interviewing Gen Xers

I am going to make a few assumptions here. I am going to assume that you have seen at least a point or two in this book that you recognize as valid. My expectations are not so lofty as to think you agree with me across the board, especially on management styles. But I am going to assume you will try to shift your management technique, if ever so slightly, to meet the different needs of Gen Xers. You OK with that?

If that is the case, then let's make sure we address these issues not only as they apply to retaining and maximizing the potential Gen Xers, but also in attracting them to our place of business as well. Does that make sense? Remember the quote about the *Inc 500*, and 30 CEOs at or under the age of 30? And I told you that many of them "get it"?

Our organizations need to be competitive in the way we attract quality Gen Xers as well as being competitive in the sales and marketing arena. The facts are that many companies have already started making many of the changes we have discussed so far. And we need to get your group up to speed.

Let's assume that you consider the Ambassador Program, or the Exchange Program or the QBM, the Weekly Observation Sheets, or better yet, others you and your teams have developed or will develop. Then why not take full advantage of what you have accomplished. Introduce those programs to Gen Xers as early as the interview period?

I just put on my glasses and re-read the Old Schooler's Management Handbook, from cover to cover, and I searched high and I searched low for the page that says these types of programs need to remain confidential during the interview process. That page was not to be found, at least not by me.

Here are the givens: We know that Gen Xers have little or no trust in corporate America. And we are beginning to understand why they feel that way. We also know that by establishing equity and empowerment in our Gen Xers, we have a better chance of developing trust and loyalty. Let's use it to attract the best Gen Xers we possibly can attract to our organizations. Or maybe you think it is a better testament to your management style not to attract the brightest employees, and instead rely on your management experience, which would make some of you experts in mediocrity. Can you say Wanna-Be?

If you are feeling really open-minded, I am going to put you to the test. Where does it say in your management handbook that the top manager has to conduct all of the interviews? Is it because of your extensive formal training in the interview process? Just how much formal training in interviews have you had? Or is it because you have had so much experience? Or you are the best at reading people?

Got ya! Then why are you having such a hard time with Gen X? It is because they are different than you are; I thought we covered that. Sorry to be abrasive but I am passionate about this point.

Can you imagine the effect on the Gen X candidate of another Gen Xer, talking about employee equity and empowerment in your company, and listing the examples? Talk about empowerment; are you strong enough to let go? Isn't that really what management is all about?

Maybe in my ranting you missed my subtle point about training for interviews. Do all of your managers or HR people work off of the same checklist? Maybe that will be the next book, but please, let's make sure everyone is talking about the programs that our company offers to meet the needs of the Gen Xers, at the very least.

Time to move on. We are almost done.

Orientation

Recently I have tried preaching to different management teams about culture. For some reason there just does not seem to be a lot of interest in corporate cultures. Then why is it such a big deal to me?

Maybe it is due to the time I spent at Yamaha and witnessed how domestic and foreign corporate cultures could be radically different, but then yet meet the same basic emotional needs of employees. Or maybe it is just that I visit so many different cultures and leadership styles in my workshops, while most managers only experience a few different cultures. Or maybe I am more sensitive to the potential differences and the advantages of some versus others. I just don't know.

What I do know is that the elements of equity and empowerment are dynamic influences over Gen X employees. So much so that the shifts in corporate management paradigms I have been describing need to go beyond a program here and there to become inherent elements in our corporate culture. This would mean that they are present in every facet of the organization. Most importantly, they need to be introduced and be significant from Day One in the corporate life of the employee.

It is time for another metaphor. When I was researching my thesis for my MBA, Management Training in Small and Medium-Sized Companies, I spent a lot of time analyzing the culture at The Walt Disney Company in Orlando, including their management training programs.

I was enamored by the way they were able to change the language, change the mindset, and transform an hourly job into an employee experience, if that makes any sense. From the first day at work, the management team at Disney started to instill their unique culture into the employees. Even back in those days, the late 80s, they not only recognized the value, but also insisted on changing the mindset of the workers to be consistent with their objectives.

On the first day, employees were expected to know the history of Mickey Mouse and the names of the Seven Dwarfs. And when I refer to employees, I am talking about custodial, maintenance, characters that did not even speak, and yes, even the executives. Every employee; can you imagine? What a great example of 100% participation.

Compare that to the cultural introduction a new hire experiences on his or her first day of work at your company. Potentially it may be the difference between a mouse and a duck. No offense to Donald of course.

I was touched by another example as well. When my daughter decided to go to Georgia Southern University, we signed up for the mandatory orientation weekend. I went with my daughter, reluctantly. Actually if the truth were to be known, I went kicking and screaming.

During the weekend they had skits and speakers; they had tours and elective sessions of information in specific categories. It was well planned, and well executed. All geared to make the incoming freshman feel welcome and part of the family. The schedule was fast and furious, and interesting, really interesting. Talk about sound bytes. They gave quick interesting snapshots of programs. See, they understand the Millennial students, and what makes them tick. They also understand the relationship between orientation and culture.

Compare that to your new hire's first day on the job. I am not suggesting a three-day dog and pony weekend in Statesboro, Georgia. But I am asking the question, what can we learn from this experience?

Now remember the Gen Xer. They process information quickly, in sound bytes, and then move on. That first day at work is critical and will set the tone for the long term. I encourage you to take a look at your orientation process from an entirely new perspective – the perspective of the Gen Xer. And, potentially, you can enhance the first-day experience and provide equity to other employees, all at the same time. Can you see where I am going with this?

Orientation Ideas

Do you believe in first impressions? How long do they last? Do you believe that they are accurate? If you answered yes, then the next question is how do we make first impressions work for us in dealing with a Gen X new hire?

First, arrange for all new hires to start on the same day if possible. Mondays or Fridays are optimum, and have your new hires experience the process as a team. If you are a smaller company and cannot afford to wait a week to get a team together, then make a team of at least two new hires; even that is better than solo. Before you judge me or dismiss this concept as unrealistic, finish the section.

This is going to sound simplistic to you when you first read it, but stay with me, it can be powerful. If you have a promotional video, shorter is better; play it for the new hire. Remember, use short sound bytes of information. If you have a television spot or radio commercials, now, on Day One, is the time to play them for the new hire. If you do not have a video, then try a scrapbook. I am not talking about a kiddie-meal scrapbook, but one of those quarter-pounder types, those three-foot-high scrapbooks.

Have each department make contributions (participation), a welcome card from senior management addressed to the name of the new hire (management support), or better yet, a welcome card signed by all of the employees in the department.

Then fill the giant scrapbook with press releases, website images, photos of events, articles written by employees, departmental photos. Fill it with images that represent your success, and your people. And keep it updated. The cost is minimal, but the image will stay in the head of the new Gen X Employee forever. The scrapbook is better than a lecture or tour, and the pictures graphically illustrate the culture of your organization.

Three years or more later, employees can still remember not only the images in the scrapbook but the person who turned the pages and took them through the book. Make sure this person knows about everything in the scrapbook. Having a Volume 1 and Volume 2 is also acceptable; just keep the exercise to 15 minutes. Remember, sound bytes.

Explain to all of your existing employees how critical the first day can be. I do not suggest we make it a party, but the fact is, that it *is* an event in the mind of the new hire. Remember Georgia Southern? Is it that much different, really, in terms of the anxieties of the new hire? Do you see the parallels?

You might try implementing an orientation team representing all departments. Each department designates a representative, and that gives us 100% participation and equity in the process. I do not want to disrespect those in the HR department; I just think we need to re-invent the orientation process for Gen X Employees. It needs to be a non-management, a peer group experience.

Have each delegate present just five to ten minutes about his department, complete with literature or achievements. Pictures are critical. And rotate the orientation delegate every month, or every three months; keep it fresh for everyone. The program needs to be concise, well-organized and brisk. This is another strong argument for singling out a single day for new hires to start.

I can hear you: "If they are here for a week and then we put them with a group, it is the same thing." No, it isn't, and you would be wrong. Can you remember your seventh day with your company? If logistics are still a concern, do the orientation on a Saturday morning two weeks before their actual first day. Or you might possibly try a 7:00 p.m. orientation during the week, for two hours.

Sooner than the first day is better than a few days later, please trust me on this.

As a matter of fact, I recommend you do this before they go to HR to fill out their exemption papers, before they shake hands with the office pool, even before we identify the rest rooms or the time clock. *Tell me when is it too early to start a culture of success?*

The desired result is for the employee to field his or her first telephone call, with the positive culture of the company tattooed in their brain. The result is a culture of a success. This will instill pride in the organization, from the first hour, on the first day, and set the standards of success high above the norm of just another "McJob".

If it works for Mickey it can work for you. It is not complicated, nor is it expensive, but it will make a difference. These types of activities do not need to be limited to big corporations. Let your employees be creative.

If you want to take it to the next level, try a follow-up meeting every quarter including all of the new hires and ask them for their input on how to make the orientation program even better. Who would know better than this group about how to improve the process? *Now we have another teambuilding question, as well as the Gen Xer's first exposure to equity in the systems of the company. Awesome!*

Chapter 21

Liberal management? I don't think so...

Liberal Management?

The following comments may surprise you. After previewing the original draft of this manuscript with my friends in senior management positions around the country, I needed to add these important thoughts to the book in response to their questions.

Some of you may have interpreted my data, opinions and vehicles as a movement towards a more liberal style of management. I am not talking about liberal management but instead management that works with people. Not in the sense the employees and middle managers now need to run the company or the organization. Employee Equity is a process for success, not a replacement for leadership.

But leadership will have to evolve. Do you understand the difference?

It is imperative that the senior managers manage the business. After all, that is what they are meant to do. My thoughts and programs are designed to make organizations more successful by reducing management frustrations with Gen Xers, minimizing the many costs of employee turnover, and maximizing the potential of Gen X Managers and Employees.

Strong management is still a paramount variable in the equation of organizational prosperity. But your mission is to get everyone on the same page, not necessarily write every single word on that page.

The Role of Management

But the styles of management and communication will have to change. Each of the programs in the final section should be launched with a critically important meeting about "interdependence", communication and the *clear definition of roles.* Communication about expectations and roles is critical to success.

The meetings would include a specific discussion on the role of senior management, as well as your expectations of the middle managers and employees. I believe the role of management is to make the final decisions in the direction of the company.

Equity is critical, but so is leadership. Be clear in your communication that we need their power, their involvement and we need their creativity. We need their direct and sincere involvement in the process and the potential solutions/improvements. That is the role of the employees.

Management still needs to define and communicate the standards of the organization, and steer the ship. You will be tested, maybe even more than before. Employees will be watching to see if everyone is evaluated to the same set of standards. They may question you at every turn. It is not insubordination it is their culture. Please understand the difference.

In the tech team story, we as managers failed to set and communicate the standards, and provide solutions to potential problems. Once the standards are clearly communicated there also must be discipline, and that too is your responsibility. And therein lies the difference.

But remember the primary role of management is to manage the truth, open the creativity and *direct* the power.

Wrap Up

So, now you have all of the elements. We discussed the characteristics of Gen Xers and the characteristics of Managers. And I tried to bring the two areas together in the final section by giving you actual tools to be implemented, as early as tomorrow morning in your business.

You might want to do a quick analysis of your existing programs or your own management style, and how they measure up against the vehicles we have discussed. In your own mind, quickly rank your employee programs or vehicles from 1 to 5, with a score of 5 being the highest. Attack the weakest areas first.

- Management Support	1	2	3	4	5
- Minimal Budget Expense	1	2	3	4	5
- Positive Reinforcement Elements	1	2	3	4	5
- 100% Participation	1	2	3	4	5
- Equity and Empowerment	1	2	3	4	5

Have we established need?

This list is not presented as comprehensive, but it is a good place to start. Remember the horse: Start by explaining why water is important, and sit back. Your only real responsibility after that is positive reinforcement, support, and above all else, truth.

I hope there are some programs or at the very least, elements of programs you found interesting. But at the end of the day, it simply boils down to honesty and truth in management. Many of you will have read with interest, but will not implement the programs. Let me make it simple for you.

Daily Goals

Make a goal for yourself. Each day at work, issue two positive reinforcement comments in the morning, and two in the afternoon. And each day offer at least two honest comments with a positive connotation regarding your expectations. Is that acceptable?

Truth builds trust, and trust builds loyalty. Do not be afraid to be honest with your group about your anxieties concerning change. If you are sincere, they will understand. Do not be afraid to talk about needing their help; but do it honestly.

If you want to email me with questions, I am OK with that, http://www.mxmuetzel.com but please do not ask me for copies of forms or program outlines, because they will mean so much more if your employees creatively develop them.

I think you have it.

Chapter 22

Final thoughts

I t is a paradox: I am closing this book, and I am not sure where to begin. I have tried to say so much to you in such a short period of time, and I am sure it will take a while to digest it all, for both of us. That is why it may be described as a handbook. Please come back, reference and visit. Believe it or not, it has had a larger impact on me than it may have had on you. Some of you will not understand that, but some of you will. I have attempted to keep you involved, to give you equity in the ideas, and to empower you to action. But change is not easy.

And yes, Mr. Covey, I do believe in interdependence for employees, a level that is two million miles beyond independence, where there is understanding in management. And although some may call me foolish, idealistic and naive, I know in my heart successful organizations will get there.

I have tried to shed some light on the differences in people and give you some background on employees you may have thought were made up of a radically different fabric than you had ever seen before. They are really not that different, just jaded, and who could blame them. The world was a different place for them than it was for you and me. I am not saying better or worse, just different.

One person, just one manager, in just one company needs to demonstrate through his or her management techniques that not all companies or managers are untrustworthy. Managers need to step up and treat their employees like they are individual assets, worth their weight in gold. Trust your instincts, and trust your employees. If you are the one to make this investment in the future of your Managers and Employees, you will reap dividends that stretch beyond the rainbow. I truly hope it is you.

If you understood my message, then I am truly blessed. Communication and empathy are gifts I never deserved but were freely given to me, and I am thankful. You have been blessed with spiritual gifts as well, and it is time to use them.

Finally, I want to apologize to you. I want to apologize for attempting to fool you into thinking this book was about Gen X Managers and Gen X Employees. It was a sorry attempt at sleight of hand. This book was not really about Gen Xers at all.

You see it is not just about them. It is also about us. People like you and me, people we work with, people we understand, and people we do not understand. That is what the book was really about.

This is a book for managers.

God bless. m

Special Thanks

I want to thank Alice, Melissa and Abbey, my family, for their undying help and support, and for sacrificing the holidays as I worked in the cave. Their loyalty to me has been inspirational. I also want to thank my dear friend, Mike Mitton, who also worked on this project and stayed with me through the dark times. Thanks to my father, a truly great manager, ahead of his time, and to my mother, bless her heart. I put them through hell. Good family and good friends are also special gifts, and I love them and appreciate them.

I want to thank my many corporate teachers/ professors, Dick Nelson, John Strang and Roger Steel (SNS Properties), for their belief in me early in my career, as well as my MBA. And thanks to the management team at Yamaha Motor Corporation, for the many opportunities they afforded me, and the tremendous education in the Japanese corporate culture. Thank you Mr. Kato and Mr. Mabuchi.

There are also many who touched me, and educated me, without even realizing how they contributed to the philosophies in this book. Pastor John Weber, my friend, and Pat Akerburg, my coach, thanks for introducing me to myself again. Jim Earley, thank you for your honesty and insight. And thanks to the spirit of coach John Galipault, for teaching me about strong leadership and coaching.

I want to thank Mr. Roy Wu (The Independent Sector) for help with the contributions data, Victoria Webster, Anne Lyndrup, Alice, and Teddy Allen (awesome) for their keen eyes. I want to thank Ken Melrose (Toro), for encouraging a young kid he didn't even know, a kid interested in management training. Special thanks to Ken Blanchard, Stephen Covey, Tom Peters, Robert Waterman Jr., and Dr.

Garfield for being the pioneer authors in the early period of the management revolution or evolution, and to Daniel Goleman for carrying the message forward. I encourage all of you to read their materials.

I also want to thank my friends at North Coast Distributing, Firestone C.C., and PGA West (Joey Garon), and Yamaha Motor Manufacturing Corporation for the concepts that have developed into unique programs that have proven to be valuable management tools. And finally, I need to thank the thousands of customers, clients and business acquaintances who have taken time to share with me, and train me over the years. After all, we are products of our environments, and I have been truly lucky and blessed.

M, Atlanta, 2003

References

1. *"40% raised in single parent households"*
   Article, "Employee Loyalty Died at the Dinner Table"
   Author, Rebecca Ryan Entrepreneur Magazine, July 31, 2002
   http://www.keepyoungtalent.com/
   free_articles.cfm?articleID=61

2. *"4 to 5 more times likely to have experienced divorce... than Boomers"*
   Book, *Welcome to the Jungle, The Why Behind Generation X*
   Author, Geoffrey T. Holtz,
   St. Martin's Press; June 1995
   Copyright ©1995 by Geoffrey T. Holtz pg. 27

3. *"Generation X, tales for an accelerated culture"*
   Book, *Generation X, tales for an accelerated culture*
   Author, Douglas Coupland
   New York: St. Martin's Press, 1991

4. *"Class: a guide through the American status system"*
   Book, *Class: a guide through the American status system*
   Author, Paul Fussell; with illustrations by Martim de Avillez.
   New York: Summit Books, 1983.

5. *"We were left alone a lot...."*
   Article, Gen X stands for meaningless term
   Author, Suzy Freeman-Greene, April 27, 2002, The Age
   http://www.theage.com.au/articles/2002/04/26/
   1019441300596.html

6. *"We're people who came from divorced families...had to"*
   Article, The X factor, What makes Generation X tick?
   Entrepreneur Magazine, August 1998 Reprinted with permission
   from Entrepreneur Media, Inc. www.entrepreneur.com
   Author, Debra Phillips, interview with Meredith Bagby, author,
   Rational Exuberance: The Influence of Generation X on the New
   American Economy, (Dutton)
   http://www.entrepreneur.com/Magazines/
   Copy_of_MA_SegArticle/0,4453,229098——1-,0(...

7. *"55% married, 7% living with someone, 65% Gen X Women"*
    Article, Where Gen X, Volunteer Today, April 2002
    http://www.volunteertoday.com/April02recrui.html

8. *"Gen Xers learn 4-5 new software titles each year"*
    Article, Stop Brain Drain
    Author, Rebecca Ryan, May 28, 2001, hot jobs cool communities
    http://www.hotjobs-coolcommunities.com/news/articles/
    artcle.cfm?ArticleID=27

9. *"Most Gen Xers leave their jobs within 18 months"*
    Article, Ca$h In on Generation X
    Author, Rebecca Morgan www.rebeccaspeaks.com
    Found in C.K. Brit Human Resource -Articles
    http://www.ckbrit-humanresources.com/articlegenx.htm

10. *"Generation X, more than 32% non-white members"*
    Article, The Millennial Generation is No Gen X
    Author, Neil Murray, San Diego Metropolitan, March 2001
    http://www.sandiegomtro.com/2001/mar/career.html

11. *"40% raised in single parent households"*
    Article, "Employee Loyalty Died at the Dinner Table"
    Author, Rebecca Ryan July 31, 2002 Entrepreneur Magazine
    http://www.keepyoungtalent.com/
    free_articles.cfm?articleID=61

12. *"40% attend worship twice a month"*
    "25% have confidence in religion"
    "47% said church teaching were important."
    Article, Generation X keeping the faith
    Author, Associated Press, Beloit Daily News, January 18, 1997
    http://www.beloitdailynews.com/197/3rel18.htm

13. *" In the 1980's GM, IBM, AT&T, US West and others cut"*
    Article, "Employee Loyalty Died at the Dinner Table"
    Author, Rebecca Ryan July 31, 2002 Entrepreneur Magazine
    http://www.keepyoungtalent.com/
    free_articles.cfm?articleID=61

14. *"Not only did almost half of voting Gen Xers, Ventura"*
Article, Gen X Finding Its Voice
Author, Carrie Lips, originally appeared in Jacksonville Journal-Courier, December 29, 1998, the Cato Institute
Referenced in http://www.socialsecurity.org/pubs/aerticles/cl-12-29-98.html

15. *"This generation has largely written off Social Security"*
Article, Gen X Finding Its Voice
Author, Carrie Lips, originally appeared in Jacksonville Journal-Courier, December 29, 1998, the Cato Institute
Referenced in http://www.socialsecurity.org/pubs/aerticles/cl-12-29-98.html

16. *"They had a better chance of seeing a UFO, than a check"*
Article, Study, Gen X
Author, Cayman Seacrest, University of Colorado, 1996
http://www.cc.colorado.edu/Dept/EC/generationx96/genx

17. *" a different set of attitudes about the workplace…"*
Article, Why can't boomers and Gen X, just get along, found in Microsoft bcentral®, Marketing Intelligence
Author, Joanna L. Krotz, Microsoft bCentral columnist, Where she references a quote from Jay A. Conger of the London Business School in his article, "How Gen X Managers Manage"
http://www.bcentral.com/articles/krotz/157.asp

18. *"But it is more than peanut butter that motivates"*
Article, Gen X Changes the Rules, Northwest Legal Search Website
Author, Linda Green Pierce, President, Northwest Legal Search, Inc
http://www.nwlegalsearch.com/articles/generation_x.html

19. *" 56% volunteered, University of Colorado, 1996…"*
Article, Study, Gen X
Author, Cayman Seacrest, University of Colorado, 1996
http://www.cc.colorado.edu/Dept/EC/generationx96/genx

20. *"Independent Sector Giving Statistics"*
Independent Sector, a diverse group of more than 1 million charitable, educational, religious, health, and social welfare organizations. Study: Recent Giving and Volunteering in the United States, 2001, Based on 4,000, adults surveyed... Special thanks to Mr. Roy Wu
http://www.IndependentSector.org, Washington DC

21. *"They've been derided as slackers, disloyal and lazy, but guess what?"*
Article, The Coming of Gen X Bosses, They're ready for management roles—but are you ready for them? Entrepreneur Magazine, November 1999
Author, Robert McGarvey rjm@mcgarvey.net
http://www.Entrepreneur.com/article/0,4621,231444,00.html

22. *" Gen X population is approximately 10%, less than boomers."*
Data taken from US Bureau of Census, International Data Base
My assumptions for comparison were based on the 2000 US census, comparing the age brackets, 20 – 34 (59.0 million) against ages, 40 – 54, (65.4 million)
http://blue.census.gov/cgi-bin/ipc/idbagg

23. *" Managerial pool shortfalls... fewer people, more jobs"*
Article, Demographics are Destiny, hot jobs, cool communities, October 18, 2002
Author, Rebecca Ryan
http://www.hotjobs-coolcommunities.com/news/articles/article.cfm?ArticleID=81

24. *" A commanding style of leadership..."*
Book, *Primal Leadership, Realizing the Power of Emotional Intelligence*
Authors, Daniel Goleman, Richard Boyatzis, Annie McKee
Harvard Business School Press, Copyright © 2002 by Daniel Goleman pg. 76

25. *"artificial harmony in management teams..."*
Book, *The Five Dysfunctions of a Team*
Author, Patrick Lencioni
Jossey-Bass, A Wiley Company Copyright
©2002 by Patrick Lencioni, pg. 91

26. *"In Search of Excellence"*
Book,*"In Search of Excellence*
Authors, Thomas J. Peters and Robert H. Waterman Jr.
HarperCollins, 1982

27. *" better environment, more productivity..."*
Book, *Primal Leadership, Realizing the Power of Emotional Intelligence*
Authors, Daniel Goleman, Richard Boyatzis, Annie McKee
Harvard Business School Press, Copyright © 2002 by Daniel
Goleman, Pg. 15

28. *"leading CEO's under age 30, Inc Magazine..."*
Article, The Next Generation, Profile of the 30 Inc 500 CEO's Who
are age 30 or younger, Inc Magazine, October 01, 1992
Author, Bruce G. Posner, http://www.inc.com/magazine/
19921001/4336.html

29. *" great service companies invest in employees success..."*
Book, *Discovering the Soul of Service*
Author, Leonard L. Berry
The Free Press, a division of Simon & Schuster Inc.
Copyright ©1999 by Leonard L. Berry, Pg. 156

30. *" Trust between the trainer and the whale..."*
Book, *Whale Done, The Power of Positive Relationships*
Authors, Ken Blanchard, Thad Lacinak, Chuck Tompkins, and
Jim Ballard, The Free Press, a division of Simon & Schuster Inc.
Copyright © 2002 Blanchard Family Partnership, Pg. 7

31. *" management techniques..."*
Book, *The 7 Habits of Highly Effective People, Powerful Lessons in
Personal Change*
Author, Stephen R. Covey
Fireside, a registered trademark of Simon & Schuster Inc.
Copyright © 1989 by Stephen R. Covey, used with permission

32. " *Interdependence…*"
   Book, *The 7 Habits of Highly Effective People, Powerful Lessons in Personal Change*
   Author, Stephen R. Covey
   Fireside, a registered trademark of Simon & Schuster Inc.
   Copyright © 1989 by Stephen R. Covey, used with permission
   Pg. 185 – 203

Visit our website, or email me with comments on the book, or interest in some of our other products....

Thanks again, Mike
http://www.mxmuetzel.com
mxmm@bellsouth.net

Quick Order Form

Yes, Please send me _____ copies of *"They're Not Aloof... Just Generation X"*, at $ 19.95 each, plus $ 4.00 for shipping and handling per book. (Georgia residents please add $ 1.00 sales tax per book) Canadian orders can be sent via money orders, and must be in US Funds. Contact us via email for special quantity discounts.

Yes, Please send me _____ copies of the *Management Solutions Training Workbook,* including time lines, sample forms, and outlines for Employee Ambassador and Employee Exchange Programs at $ 49.95 each, plus $ 4.00 for shipping and handling per book. (Georgia residents please add $ 2.50 sales tax per workbook)

Yes, Please send me _____ copies of the book on audiocassette at: $ 19.95 each, plus $ 4.00 for shipping and handling per set. (Georgia residents please add $ 1.00 sales tax per audio set)

My check or money order for $ _____ is enclosed.

Please charge my: _____Visa _____Master Card _____American Express

❑ I am interested having Michael Muetzel speak to our corporation or organization.

Name _____

Credit Card Number _____

Organization _____

Address _____

City / State/ Zip _____

Phone _____ Email _____

Exp. Date _____ Signature _____

Fax to Mx Marketing, 770-486-1419 or **Please make your check payable to:**

Steel Bay Publishing
6007 Financial Plaza, Suite 510
Shreveport, LA 71129

To purchase on line: **http://www.mxmuetzel.com**

Notes...

Notes...